FREE DVD   FREE   FREE DVD

From Stress to Success DVD from Trivium Test Prep

Dear Customer,

Thank you for purchasing from Trivium Test Prep! Whether you're looking to join the military, get into college, or advance your career, we're honored to be a part of your journey.

To show our appreciation (and to help you relieve a little of that test-prep stress), we're offering a **FREE *TABE Essential Test Tips DVD*** by Trivium Test Prep. Our DVD includes 35 test preparation strategies that will help keep you calm and collected before and during your big exam. All we ask is that you email us your feedback and describe your experience with our product. Amazing, awful, or just so-so: we want to hear what you have to say!

To receive your **FREE *TABE Essential Test Tips DVD***, please email us at 5star@triviumtestprep. com. Include "Free 5 Star" in the subject line and the following information in your email:

1. The title of the product you purchased.
2. Your rating from 1 – 5 (with 5 being the best).
3. Your feedback about the product, including how our materials helped you meet your goals and ways in which we can improve our products.
4. Your full name and shipping address so we can send your **FREE *TABE Essential Test Tips DVD***.

If you have any questions or concerns please feel free to contact us directly at 5star@triviumtestprep.com.

Thank you, and good luck with your studies!

* Please note that the free DVD is <u>not included</u> with this book. To receive the free DVD, please follow the instructions above.

TABE Test Study Guide:

TABE 11/12 Exam Prep Book with Practice Questions

ELISSA SIMON

TABLE OF CONTENTS

INTRODUCTION

The fact that you've purchased this book means two things. The first is that you're preparing for, or at least considering taking, the TABE exam, which can open new doors for your future by greatly expanding your options for careers. The second is that you've already taken an excellent first step in picking up this study guide.

We'll provide you with a detailed overview of the TABE, so that you know exactly what to expect on test day, then we'll cover all of the subjects over which you will be tested, providing multiple practice sections for you to test your knowledge and improve. Even if it's been a while since your last major examination, don't worry; we'll make sure you're more than ready!

WHAT IS THE TABE?

The TABE exam measures your skills through the high school level in Language Arts, Reading, and Mathematics. In short, it tests everything taught in high school, so employers and institutions will know that you are prepared for new training.

Reading

50 questions, 50 minute time limit. Tests ability to read and interpret written passages.

Mathematics

There are 2 separate math sections on the TABE, however, for purposes of studying we will cover it in one chapter. While the presentation of questions is slightly different in each section, it really does not matter how the question is posed if you understand the fundamentals of math. It always comes down to adding, subtracting, multiplying, and dividing.

- Math Comprehension: 40 questions, 25 minute time limit.
- Math Application: 50 questions, 50 minute time limit.

Language, Language Mechanics, Vocabulary, Spelling

Tests knowledge of sentence structure, usage, mechanics, grammar, and organization. For purposes of this study guide, all sections are taught together. As you know, language, spelling, and vocabulary are all connected. Only the Language section is required; Language Mechanics, Vocabulary, and Spelling are optional.

- Language: 55 questions, 55 minute time limit.

- Language Mechanics (optional section): 20 questions, 14 minute time limit
- Vocabulary (optional section): 20 questions, 15 minute time limit.
- Spelling (optional section): 20 questions, 10 minute time limit.

SCORING

There is no set passing or failing score on the TABE. You will need to check with the school or employment agency to find out what their minimum standards are. The scoring criteria is rather complicated, requiring a few different charts for each section. For many people, if you can get 70% of more of the question correct while working through this book, you should do fine.

HOW THIS BOOK WORKS

The subsequent chapters in this book are divided into a review of those topics covered on the exam. This is not to "teach" or "re-teach" you these concepts – there is no way to cram all of that material into one book! Instead, we are going to help you recall all of the information that you've already learned. Even more importantly, we'll show you how to apply that knowledge.

Each chapter includes an extensive review, with practice drills at the end to test your knowledge. With time, practice, and determination, you'll be completely prepared for test day.

READING

THE MAIN IDEA

The **MAIN IDEA** of a text is the argument that the author is trying to make about a particular **TOPIC**. Every sentence in a passage should support or address the main idea in some way.

Identifying the Main Idea

Consider a political election. A candidate is running for office and plans to deliver a speech asserting her position on tax reform, which is that taxes should be lowered. The topic of the speech is tax reform, and the main idea is that taxes should be lowered. The candidate is going to assert this in her speech, and support it with examples proving why lowering taxes would benefit the public and how it could be accomplished.

> ⚠ **Topic**: The subject of the passage. **Main idea**: The argument the writer is making about the topic.

Other candidates may have different perspectives on the same topic; they may believe that higher taxes are necessary, or that current taxes are adequate. It is likely that their speeches, while on the same topic of tax reform, would have different main ideas supported by different examples and evidence.

Let's look at an example passage to see how to identify the topic and main idea.

> Babe Didrikson Zaharias, one of the most decorated female athletes of the twentieth century, is an inspiration for everyone. Born in 1911 in Beaumont, Texas, Zaharias lived in a time when women were considered second class to men, but she never let that stop her from becoming a champion. Zaharias was one of seven children in a poor immigrant family and was competitive from an early age. As a child she excelled at most things she tried, especially sports, which continued into high school and beyond. After high school, Zaharias played amateur basketball for two years, and soon after began training in track and field. Despite the fact that women were only allowed to enter in three events, Zaharias represented the United States in the 1932 Los Angeles Olympics, and won two gold medals and one silver in track and field events.

The topic of this paragraph is obviously Babe Zaharias—the whole passage describes events from her life. Determining the main idea, however, requires a little more analysis. To figure out the main idea, consider what the writer is saying about Zaharias. The passage describes her life, but the main idea of the paragraph is what it says about her accomplishments. The writer is saying that she is someone to admire. That is the main idea and what unites all the information in the paragraph.

Example

From so far away it's easy to imagine the surface of our solar system's planets as enigmas—how could we ever know what those far-flung planets really look like? It turns out, however, that scientists have a number of tools at their disposal that allow them to paint detailed pictures of many planets' surfaces. The topography of Venus, for example, has been explored by several space probes, including the Russian Venera landers and NASA's *Magellan* orbiter. In addition to these long-range probes, NASA has also used its series of "Great Observatories" to study distant planets. These four massively powerful orbiting telescopes are the famous Hubble Space Telescope, the Compton Gamma Ray Observatory, the Chandra X-Ray Observatory, and the Spitzer Space Telescope. Such powerful telescopes aren't just found in space: NASA makes use of Earth-based telescopes as well. Scientists at the National Radio Astronomy Observatory in Charlottesville, Virginia, have spent decades using radio imaging to build an incredibly detailed portrait of Venus's surface.

Which of the following sentences best describes the main idea of the passage?

A) It's impossible to know what the surfaces of other planets are really like.

B) Telescopes are an important tool for scientists studying planets in our solar system.

C) Venus's surface has many of the same features as Earth's, including volcanoes, craters, and channels.

D) Scientists use a variety of advanced technologies to study the surfaces of the planets in our solar system.

Answer:

D) is correct. Choice A can be eliminated because it directly contradicts the rest of the passage. Choices B and C can also be eliminated because they offer only specific details from the passage. While both choices contain details from the passage, neither is general enough to encompass the passage as a whole. Only choice D provides an assertion that is both backed up by the passage's content and general enough to cover the entire passage.

Topic and Summary Sentences

The topic, and sometimes the main idea of a paragraph, is introduced in the TOPIC SENTENCE. The topic sentence usually appears early in a passage. The first sentence in the example paragraph about Babe Zaharias states the topic and main idea: *Babe Didrikson Zaharias, one of the most decorated female athletes of the twentieth century, is an inspiration for everyone.*

Even though paragraphs generally begin with topic sentences, on occasion writers build up to the topic sentence by using supporting details in order to generate interest or construct an argument. Be alert for paragraphs in which writers do not include a clear topic sentence.

There may also be a **SUMMARY SENTENCE** at the end of a passage. As its name suggests, this sentence sums up the passage, often by restating the main idea and the author's key evidence supporting it.

Example

The Constitution of the United States establishes a series of limits to rein in centralized power. "Separation of powers" distributes federal authority among three branches: the executive, the legislative, and the judicial. "Checks and balances" allow the branches to prevent any one branch from usurping power. "States' rights" are protected under the Constitution from too much encroachment by the federal government. "Enumeration of powers" names the specific and few powers the federal government has. These four restrictions have helped sustain the American republic for over two centuries.

Which of the following is the passage's topic sentence?

A) These four restrictions have helped sustain the American republic for over two centuries.

B) The Constitution of the United States establishes a series of limits to rein in centralized power.

C) "Enumeration of powers" names the specific and few powers the federal government has.

D) "Checks and balances" allow the branches to prevent any one branch from usurping power.

Answer:

B) is correct. Choice B is the first sentence of the passage and introduces the topic. Choice A is the final sentence of the passage and summarizes the passage's content. Choices C and D are supporting sentences found within the body of the passage. They include important details that support the main idea of the passage.

SUPPORTING DETAILS

SUPPORTING DETAILS reinforce the author's main idea. Let's look again at the passage about athlete Babe Zaharias.

Babe Didrikson Zaharias, one of the most decorated female athletes of the twentieth century, is an inspiration for everyone. Born in 1911 in Beaumont, Texas, Zaharias lived in a time when women were considered second class to men, but she never let that stop her from becoming a champion. Babe was one of seven children in a poor immigrant family and was competitive from an early age. As a child she excelled at most things she tried, especially sports, which continued into high school and beyond. After high school, Babe played amateur basketball for two years, and soon after began training in track and field. Despite the fact that women were only allowed to enter in three events, Zaharias represented the United States in the 1932 Los Angeles Olympics, and won two gold medals and one silver for track and field events.

Remember that the main idea of the passage is that Zaharias is someone to admire—an idea introduced in the opening sentence. The remainder of the paragraph provides details that support this assertion. These details include the circumstances of her childhood, her childhood success at sports, and the medals she won at the Olympics.

Signal words: *for example, specifically, in addition, furthermore, for instance, others, in particular, some*

When looking for supporting details, be alert for SIGNAL WORDS. These signal words tell you that a supporting fact or idea will follow, and so can be helpful in identifying supporting details. Signal words can also help you rule out certain sentences as the main idea or topic sentence. If a sentence begins with one of these phrases, it will likely be too specific to be a main idea.

Examples

From so far away it's easy to imagine the surface of our solar system's planets as enigmas—how could we ever know what those far-flung planets really look like? It turns out, however, that scientists have a number of tools at their disposal that allow them to paint detailed pictures of many planets' surfaces. The topography of Venus, for example, has been explored by several space probes, including the Russian Venera landers and NASA's *Magellan* orbiter. In addition to these long-range probes, NASA has also used its series of orbiting telescopes to study distant planets. These four massively powerful telescopes include the famous Hubble Space Telescope as well as the Compton Gamma Ray Observatory, the Chandra X-Ray Observatory, and the Spitzer Space Telescope. Such powerful telescopes aren't just found in space: NASA makes use of Earth-based telescopes as well. Scientists at the National Radio Astronomy Observatory in Charlottesville, Virginia, have spent decades using radio imaging to build an incredibly detailed portrait of Venus's surface.

1. According to the passage, which of the following is a space probe used to explore the surface of Venus?

   A) *Magellan* orbiter

   B) Hubble Space Telescope

   C) Spitzer Space Telescope

   D) National Radio Astronomy Observatory

   Answer:

   A) is correct. The passage states, "The topography of Venus, for example, has been explored by several space probes, including the Russian Venera landers and NASA's *Magellan* orbiter." The other choices are mentioned in the passage, but are not space probes.

2. If true, which detail could be added to the passage above to support the author's argument that scientists use many different technologies to study the surface of planets?

   A) Because Earth's atmosphere blocks X-rays, gamma rays, and infrared radiation, NASA needed to put telescopes in orbit above the atmosphere.

   B) In 2015, NASA released a map of Venus that was created by compiling images from orbiting telescopes and long-range space probes.

   C) NASA is currently using the *Curiosity* and *Opportunity* rovers to look for signs of ancient life on Mars.

   D) NASA has spent over $2.5 billion to build, launch, and repair the Hubble Space Telescope.

Answer:

B) is correct. Choice B is the best option because it addresses the use of multiple technologies to study the surface of planets. Choices C and D can be eliminated because they do not address the topic of studying the surface of planets. Choice A can also be eliminated because it only addresses a single technology.

The Author's Purpose

Whenever an author writes a text, she always has a purpose, whether that's to entertain, inform, explain, or persuade. A short story, for example, is meant to entertain, while an online news article would be designed to inform the public about a current event.

Each of these different types of writing has a specific name. On the CHSPE, you will be asked to identify which of these categories a passage fits into:

- Narrative writing tells a story. (novel, short story, play)
- Expository writing informs people. (newspaper and magazine articles)
- Technical writing explains something. (product manual, directions)
- Persuasive writing tries to convince the reader of something. (opinion column on a blog)

You may also be asked about primary and secondary sources. These terms describe not the writing itself but the author's relationship to what's being written about. A PRIMARY SOURCE is an unaltered piece of writing that was composed during the time when the events being described took place; these texts are often written by the people involved. A SECONDARY SOURCE might address the same topic but provides extra commentary or analysis. These texts can be written by people not directly involved in the events. For example, a book written by a political candidate to inform people about his or her stand on an issue is a primary source; an online article written by a journalist analyzing how that position will affect the election is a secondary source.

Example

Elizabeth closed her eyes and braced herself on the armrests that divided her from her fellow passengers. Take-off was always the worst part for her. The revving of the engines, the way her stomach dropped as the plane lurched upward: it made her feel sick. Then, she had to watch the world fade away beneath her, getting smaller and smaller until it was just her and the clouds hurtling through the sky. Sometimes (but only sometimes) it just had to be endured, though. She focused on the thought of her sister's smiling face and her new baby nephew as the plane slowly pulled onto the runway."

The passage above is reflective of which type of writing?

A) Narrative

B) Expository

C) Technical

D) Persuasive

Answer:

The passage is telling a story—we meet Elizabeth and learn about her fear of flying—so it's a narrative text (answer a). There is no factual information presented or explained, nor is the author trying to persuade the reader.

FACTS VS. OPINIONS

Reading passages you might be asked to identify a statement as either a fact or an opinion.

Which of the following phrases would be associated with opinions? *for example, studies have shown, I believe, in fact, it's possible that*

A **FACT** is a statement or thought that can be proven to be true. The statement *Wednesday comes after Tuesday* is a fact—you can point to a calendar to prove it. In contrast, an **OPINION** is an assumption, not based in fact, that cannot be proven to be true. The assertion that *television is more entertaining than feature films* is an opinion—people will disagree on this, and there is no reference you can use to prove or disprove it.

Example

Exercise is critical for healthy development in children. Today in the United States, there is an epidemic of poor childhood health; many of these children will face further illnesses in adulthood that are due to poor diet and lack of exercise now. This is a problem for all Americans, especially with the rising cost of health care.

It is vital that school systems and parents encourage children to engage in a minimum of thirty minutes of cardiovascular exercise each day, mildly increasing their heart rate for a sustained period. This is proven to decrease the likelihood of developmental diabetes, obesity, and a multitude of other health problems. Also, children need a proper diet, rich in fruits and vegetables, so they can develop physically and learn healthy eating habits early on.

Which of the following in the passage is a fact, not an opinion?

A) Fruits and vegetables are the best way to help children be healthy.

B) Children today are lazier than they were in previous generations.

C) The risk of diabetes in children is reduced by physical activity.

D) Children should engage in thirty minutes of exercise a day.

Answer:

C) is correct. Choice C is a simple fact stated by the author. It is introduced by the word *proven* to indicate that it is supported by evidence. Choice B can be discarded immediately because it is not discussed anywhere in the passage, and also because it is negative, usually a hint in multiple-choice questions that an answer choice is wrong. Choices A and D are both opinions—the author is promoting exercise, fruits, and vegetables as a way to make children healthy. (Notice that these incorrect answers contain words that hint at being an opinion such as *best* or *should*.)

MAKING INFERENCES

In addition to understanding the main idea and factual content of a passage, you will also be asked to take your analysis one step further and anticipate what other information could logically be added to the passage. In a nonfiction passage, for example, you might be asked which statement the author of the passage would agree with. In an excerpt from a fictional work, you might be asked to anticipate what the character would do next.

To answer such questions, you need to have a solid understanding of the topic and main idea of the passage. Armed with this information, you can figure out which of the answer choices best fits the criteria (or, alternatively, which do not). For example, if the author of the passage is advocating for safer working conditions in factories, any details that could be added to the passage should support that idea. You might add sentences that contain information about the number of accidents that occur in factories or that outline a new plan for fire safety.

Example

Exercise is critical for healthy development in children. Today in the United States, there is an epidemic of poor childhood health; many of these children will face further illnesses in adulthood that are due to poor diet and lack of exercise now. This is a problem for all Americans, especially with the rising cost of health care.

It is vital that school systems and parents encourage children to engage in a minimum of thirty minutes of cardiovascular exercise each day, mildly increasing their heart rate for a sustained period. This is proven to decrease the likelihood of developmental diabetes, obesity, and a multitude of other health problems. Also, children need a proper diet, rich in fruits and vegetables, so they can develop physically and learn healthy eating habits early on.

Which of the following statements might the author of this passage agree with?

A) Adults who do not have healthy eating habits should be forced to pay more for health care.

B) Schools should be required by federal law to provide vegetables with every meal.

C) Healthy eating habits can only be learned at home.

D) Schools should encourage students to bring lunches from home.

Answer:

B) is correct. Since the author argues that children need a proper diet rich in fruits and vegetables, we can infer that the author would agree with choice B. The author describes the cost of health care as a problem for all Americans, implying that he would not want to punish adults who never learned healthy eating habits (choice A). Choices C and D are contradicted by the author's focus on creating healthy habits in schools.

VOCABULARY

On the Reading section you may also be asked to provide definitions or intended meanings of words within passages. You may have never encountered some of these words before the test, but there are tricks you can use to figure out what they mean.

Context Clues

One of the most fundamental vocabulary skills is using the context in which a word is found to determine its meaning. Your ability to read sentences carefully is extremely helpful when it comes to understanding new vocabulary words.

Vocabulary questions will usually include SENTENCE CONTEXT CLUES within the sentence that contains the word. There are several clues that can help you understand the context, and therefore the meaning of a word:

RESTATEMENT CLUES state the definition of the word in the sentence. The definition is often set apart from the rest of the sentence by a comma, parentheses, or a colon.

> Teachers often prefer teaching students with <u>intrinsic</u> motivation:
> these students have an <u>internal</u> desire to learn.
>
> The meaning of *intrinsic* is restated as *internal*.

CONTRAST CLUES include the opposite meaning of a word. Words like *but, on the other hand,* and *however* are tip-offs that a sentence contains a contrast clue.

> Janet was <u>destitute</u> after she lost her job, but her wealthy
> sister helped her get back on her feet.
>
> *Destitute* is contrasted with *wealthy*, so the definition of destitute is *poor*.

POSITIVE/NEGATIVE CLUES tell you whether a word has a positive or negative meaning.

> The film was <u>lauded</u> by critics as stunning, and was nominated for
> several awards.
>
> The positive descriptions *stunning* and *nominated for several awards* suggest
> that *lauded* has a positive meaning.

Examples

Select the answer that most closely matches the definition of the underlined word or phrase as it is used in the sentence.

1. The dog was <u>dauntless</u> in the face of danger, braving the fire to save the girl trapped inside the building.

   A) difficult

   B) fearless

   C) imaginative

   D) startled

   Answer:

   B) is correct. Demonstrating bravery in the face of danger would be fearless. The restatement clue (*braving*) tells you exactly what the word means.

2. Beth did not spend any time preparing for the test, but Tyrone kept a <u>rigorous</u> study schedule.

   A) strict

   B) loose

   C) boring

   D) strange

   Answer:

   A) is correct. The word *but* tells us that Tyrone studied in a different way from Beth, which means it is a contrast clue. If Beth did not study hard, then Tyrone did. The best answer, therefore, is choice A.

Analyzing Words

As you know, determining the meaning of a word can be more complicated than just looking in a dictionary. A word might have more than one DENOTATION, or definition, and which one the author intends can only be judged by looking at the surrounding text. For example, the word *quack* can refer to the sound a duck makes or to a person who publicly pretends to have a qualification which he or she does not actually possess.

A word may also have different CONNOTATIONS, which are the implied meanings and emotions a word evokes in the reader. For example, a cubicle is simply a walled desk in an office, but for many the word implies a constrictive, uninspiring workplace. Connotations can vary greatly between cultures and even between individuals.

Last, authors might make use of FIGURATIVE LANGUAGE, which is the use of a word to imply something other than the word's literal definition. This is often done by comparing two things. If you say *I felt like a butterfly when I got a new haircut*, the listener knows you do not resemble an insect but instead felt beautiful and transformed.

Examples

Select the answer that most closely matches the definition of the underlined word or phrase as it is used in the sentence.

1. The patient's uneven <u>pupils</u> suggested that brain damage was possible.

   A) part of the eye
   B) student in a classroom
   C) walking pace
   D) breathing sounds

   Answer:

   A) is correct. Only choice A matches both the definition of the word and context of the sentence. Choice B is an alternative definition for pupil, but does not make sense in the sentence. Both C and D could be correct in the context of the sentence, but neither is a definition of pupil.

2. Aiden examined the antique lamp and worried that he had been <u>taken for a ride</u>. He had paid a lot for the vintage lamp, but it looked like it was worthless.

   A) transported
   B) forgotten
   C) deceived
   D) hindered

   Answer:

   C) is correct. It is clear from the context of the sentence that Aiden was not literally taken for a ride. Instead, this phrase is an example of figurative language. From context clues you can figure out that Aiden paid too much for the lamp, so he was deceived.

Word Structure

You are not expected to know every word in the English language for your test; rather, you will need to use deductive reasoning to find the best definition of the word in question. Many words can be broken down into three main parts to help determine their meaning:

PREFIX – ROOT – SUFFIX

ROOTS are the building blocks of all words. Every word is either a root itself or has a root. The root is what is left when you strip away the prefixes and suffixes from a word. For example, in the word *unclear*, if you take away the prefix *un–*, you have the root *clear*.

Roots are not always recognizable words, because they often come from Latin or Greek words, such as *nat*, a Latin root meaning born. The word *native*, which means a person born in a referenced place, comes from this root; so does the word *prenatal*, meaning *before birth*. It is important to keep in mind, however, that roots do not always match the original definitions of words, and they can have several different spellings.

PREFIXES are elements added to the beginning of a word, and **SUFFIXES** are elements added to the end of the word; together they are known as affixes. They carry assigned meanings and can be attached to a word to completely change the word's meaning or to enhance the word's original meaning.

> ✔
> Can you figure out the definitions of the following words using their parts? *ambidextrous, anthropology, diagram, egocentric, hemisphere, homicide, metamorphosis, nonsense, portable, rewind, submarine, triangle, unicycle*

Let's use the word *prefix* itself as an example: *fix* means to place something securely and *pre–* means before. Therefore, *prefix* means to place something before or in front of. Now let's look at a suffix: in the word *feminism*, *femin* is a root which means female. The suffix *–ism* means act, practice, or process. Thus, *feminism* is the process of establishing equal rights for women.

Although you cannot determine the meaning of a word from a prefix or suffix alone, you can use this knowledge to eliminate answer choices. Understanding whether the word is positive or negative can give you the partial meaning of the word.

Table 1.1. Common Roots

ROOT	DEFINITION	EXAMPLE
ast(er)	star	asteroid, astronomy
audi	hear	audience, audible
auto	self	automatic, autograph
bene	good	beneficent, benign
bio	life	biology, biorhythm
cap	take	capture
ced	yield	secede
chrono	time	chronometer, chronic
corp	body	corporeal
crac or crat	rule	autocrat
demo	people	democracy
dict	say	dictionary, dictation
duc	lead or make	ductile, produce
gen	give birth	generation, genetics
geo	earth	geography, geometry
grad	step	graduate
graph	write	graphical, autograph
ject	throw	eject

ROOT	DEFINITION	EXAMPLE
jur or jus	law	justice, jurisdiction
juven	young	juvenile
log or logue	thought	logic, logarithm
luc	light	lucidity
man	hand	manual
mand	order	remand
mis	send	transmission
mono	one	monotone
omni	all	omnivore
path	feel	sympathy
phil	love	philanthropy
phon	sound	phonograph
port	carry	export
qui	rest	quiet
scrib or script	write	scribe, transcript
sense or sent	feel	sentiment
tele	far away	telephone
terr	earth	terrace
uni	single	unicode
vac	empty	vacant
vid or vis	see	video, vision

Table 1.2. Common Prefixes

PREFIX	DEFINITION	EXAMPLE
a– (also an–)	not, without; to, toward; of, completely	atheist, anemic, aside, aback, anew, abashed
ante–	before, preceding	antecedent, anteroom
anti–	opposing, against	antibiotic, anticlimax
belli–	warlike, combative	belligerent, antebellum
com– (also co–, col–, con–, cor–)	with, jointly, completely	combat, cooperate, collide, confide, correspond
dis– (also di–)	negation, removal	disadvantage, disbar
en– (also em–)	put into or on; bring into the condition of; intensify	engulf, embrace
hypo–	under	hypoglycemic, hypodermic
in– (also il–, im–, ir–)	not, without; in, into, toward, inside	infertile, impossible, illegal, irregular, influence, include
intra–	inside, within	intravenous, intrapersonal
out–	surpassing, exceeding; external, away from	outperform, outdoor

Table 1.2. Common Prefixes (continued)

PREFIX	DEFINITION	EXAMPLE
over–	excessively, completely; upper, outer, over, above	overconfident, overcast
pre–	before	precondition, preadolescent, prelude
re–	again	reapply, remake
semi–	half, partly	semicircle, semiconscious
syn– (also sym–)	in union, acting together	synthesis, symbiotic
trans–	across, beyond	transdermal
trans–	into a different state	translate
under–	beneath, below; not enough	underarm, undersecretary, underdeveloped

Examples

Select the answer that most closely matches the definition of the underlined word or phrase as it is used in the sentence.

1. The <u>bellicose</u> dog will be sent to training school next week.

   A) misbehaved

   B) friendly

   C) scared

   D) aggressive

   Answer:

   D) is correct. Both *misbehaved* and *aggressive* look like possible answers given the context of the sentence. However, the prefix *belli–*, which means warlike, can be used to confirm that *aggressive* is the right answer.

2. The new menu <u>rejuvenated</u> the restaurant and made it one of the most popular spots in town.

   A) established

   B) invigorated

   C) improved

   D) motivated

   Answer:

   B) is correct. All the answer choices could make sense in the context of the sentence, so it is necessary to use word structure to find the definition. The root *juven* means young and the prefix *re–* means again, so *rejuvenate* means to be made young again. The answer choice with the most similar meaning is *invigorated*, which means to give something energy.

Read the following passages and answer the questions that correspond with each passage:

THE FLU

Influenza, or the flu, has historically been one of the most common and deadliest human sicknesses. While many people who contract this virus will recover, others will not. Over the past 150 years, tens of millions of people have died from the flu, and millions more have been left with lingering complications including secondary infections.

Although it's a common disease, the flu is actually not highly infectious; that is, it is relatively difficult to contract. The virus can only be transmitted when individuals come into direct contact with the bodily fluids of people infected with it, often when they are exposed to expelled aerosol particles resulting from coughing and sneezing. Since these particles only travel short distances and the virus will die within a few hours on hard surfaces, it can be contained with simple health measures like hand washing and face masks.

However, the spread of this disease can only be contained when people are aware that such measures must be taken. One of the reasons the flu has historically been so deadly is the window of time between a person's infection and the development of symptoms. Viral shedding—when the body releases a virus that has been successfully reproducing in it—takes place two days after infection, while symptoms do not usually develop until the third day. Thus, infected individuals may unknowingly infect others for least twenty-four hours before developing symptoms themselves.

1. What is the main idea of the passage?

   A) The flu is a deadly disease that's difficult to control because people become infectious before they show symptoms.

   B) In order for the flu to be transmitted, individuals must come in contact with bodily fluids from infected individuals.

   C) The spread of flu is easy to contain because the virus does not live long either as aerosol particles or on hard surfaces.

   D) The flu has killed tens of millions of people and can often cause deadly secondary infections.

2. Why isn't the flu considered to be highly infectious?

   A) Many people who get the flu will recover and have no lasting complications, so only a small number of people who become infected will die.

   B) The process of viral shedding takes two days, so infected individuals have enough time to implement simple health measures that stop the spread of the disease.

   C) The flu virus cannot travel far or live for long periods of time outside the human body, so its spread can easily be contained if measures are taken.

   D) Twenty-four hours is a relatively short period of time for the virus to spread among a population.

3. Which of the following correctly describes the flu?
   A) The flu is easy to contract and always fatal.
   B) The flu is difficult to contract and always fatal.
   C) The flu is easy to contract and sometimes fatal.
   D) The flu is difficult to contract and sometimes fatal.

4. Which statement is not a detail from the passage?
   A) Tens of millions of people have been killed by the flu virus.
   B) There is typically a twenty-four hour window during which individuals are infectious but not showing flu symptoms.
   C) Viral shedding is the process by which people recover from the flu.
   D) The flu can be transmitted by direct contact with bodily fluids from infected individuals or by exposure to aerosol particles.

5. What is the meaning of the word *measures* in the last paragraph?
   A) a plan of action
   B) a standard unit
   C) an adequate amount
   D) a rhythmic movement

6. What can the reader conclude from the passage above?
   A) Preemptively implementing health measures like hand washing and face masks could help stop the spread of the flu virus.
   B) Doctors are not sure how the flu virus is transmitted, so they are unsure how to stop it from spreading.
   C) The flu is dangerous because it is both deadly and highly infectious.
   D) Individuals stop being infectious three days after they are infected.

SNAKES

Skin coloration and markings play an important role in the world of snakes. Those intricate diamonds, stripes, and swirls help these animals hide from predators and attract mates. Perhaps most importantly (for us humans, anyway), the markings can also indicate whether a snake is venomous. While it might seem counterintuitive for a poisonous snake to stand out in bright red or blue, that fancy costume tells any approaching predator that eating it would be a bad idea.

If you see a flashy-looking snake out the woods, though, those markings don't necessarily mean it's poisonous: some snakes have a found a way to ward off predators without the actual venom. The California king snake, for example, has very similar markings to the venomous coral snake with whom it frequently shares a habitat. However, the king snake is actually nonvenomous; it's merely pretending to be dangerous to eat. A predatory hawk or eagle, usually hunting from high in the sky, can't tell the difference between the two species, so the king snake gets passed over and lives another day.

7. What is the author's primary purpose in writing this essay?

   A) to explain how the markings on a snake are related to whether it is venomous

   B) to teach readers the difference between coral snakes and king snakes

   C) to illustrate why snakes are dangerous

   D) to demonstrate how animals survive in difficult environments

8. What can the reader conclude from the passage above?

   A) The king snake is dangerous to humans.

   B) The coral snake and the king snake are both hunted by the same predators.

   C) It's safe to handle snakes in the woods because you can easily tell whether they're poisonous.

   D) The king snake changes its markings when hawks or eagles are close by.

9. What is the best summary of this passage?

   A) Humans can use coloration and markings to determine whether snakes are poisonous.

   B) Animals often use coloration and markings to attract mates and warn predators that they're poisonous.

   C) The California king snake and coral snake have nearly identical markings.

   D) Venomous snakes often have bright markings, although nonvenomous snakes can also mimic those colors.

10. Which statement is not a detail from the passage?

   A) Predators will avoid eating king snakes because their markings are similar to those on coral snakes.

   B) King snakes and coral snakes live in the same habitats.

   C) The coral snake uses its coloration to hide from predators.

   D) The king snake is not venomous.

11. What is the meaning of the word *intricate* in the first paragraph?

   A) complicated

   B) colorful

   C) purposeful

   D) changeable

12. What is the difference between king snakes and coral snakes according to the passage?

   A) Both king snakes and coral snakes are nonvenomous, but coral snakes have colorful markings.

   B) Both king snakes and coral snakes are venomous, but king snakes have colorful markings.

   C) King snakes are nonvenomous, while coral snakes are venomous.

   D) Coral snakes are nonvenomous, while king snakes are venomous.

TAKING TEMPERATURES

Taking a person's temperature is one of the most basic and common health care tasks. Everyone from nurses to emergency medical technicians to concerned parents has needed to grab a thermometer and take somebody's temperature. But what is the best way to get an accurate reading? The answer depends on the situation.

The most common way people measure body temperature is orally. A simple digital or disposable thermometer is placed under the tongue for a few minutes, and the task is complete. There are many situations, however, when measuring temperature orally isn't an option. For example, when a person can't breathe through his nose, he won't be able to keep his mouth closed long enough to get an accurate reading. In these situations, it's often preferable to place the thermometer in the rectum or armpit. In addition, using the rectum provides a much more accurate reading than any other location does.

It's also often the case that certain people, like agitated patients or fussy babies, won't be able to sit still long enough for an accurate reading. In these situations, it's best to use a thermometer that works much more quickly, such as one that measures temperature in the ear or at the temporal artery. No matter which method is chosen, however, it's important to check the average temperature for each region, as it can vary by several degrees.

13. Which statement is not a detail from the passage?

A) Taking someone's temperature in her ear or at her temporal artery is more accurate than taking it orally.

B) If an individual cannot breathe through his nose, taking his temperature orally will likely result in an inaccurate reading.

C) The standard human body temperature varies depending on whether it's measured in the mouth, rectum, armpit, ear, or temporal artery.

D) The most common way to measure temperature is by placing a thermometer in the mouth.

14. According to the passage, why is it sometimes preferable to take a person's temperature rectally?

A) Rectal readings are more accurate than oral readings.

B) Many people cannot sit still long enough to have their temperatures taken orally.

C) Temperature readings can vary widely between regions of the body.

D) Many people do not have access to fast-acting thermometers.

15. What is the author's primary purpose in writing this essay?

A) to advocate for the use of thermometers that measure temperature in the ear or at the temporal artery

B) to explain the methods available to measure a person's temperature and the situations in which each method is appropriate

C) to warn readers that the average temperature of the human body varies by region

D) to discuss how nurses use different types of thermometers depending on the patient they are examining

16. What is the best summary of this passage?

    A) It's important that everyone knows the best way to take a person's temperature in any given situation.

    B) The most common method of taking a person's temperature—orally—isn't appropriate in some situations.

    C) The most accurate way to take a temperature is by placing a digital thermometer in the rectum.

    D) It's important to check a person's temperature in more than one region of the body.

17. What is the meaning of the word *agitated* in the last paragraph?

    A) obviously upset

    B) quickly moving

    C) violently ill

    D) slightly dirty

CREDIT SCORES

Credit scores, which range from 300 to 850, are a single value that summarizes an individual's credit history. Pay your bills late? Your credit score will be lower than that of someone who gets their electric bill filed on the first of every month. Just paid off your massive student loans? You can expect your credit score to shoot up. The companies that compile credit scores actually keep track of all the loans, credit cards, and bill payments in your name. This massive amount of information is summed up in a credit report, which is then distilled to a single value: your credit score.

Credit scores are used by many institutions who need to evaluate the risk of providing loans, rentals, or services to individuals. Banks use credit scores when deciding when to approve loans; they can also use them to determine the terms of the loan itself. Similarly, car dealers, landlords, and credit card companies will likely all access your credit report before agreeing to do business with you. Even your employer can access a modified version of your credit report (although it will not have your actual credit score on it).

When it comes to credit, everyone begins with a clean slate. The first time you access any credit—be it a credit card, student loan, or rental agreement—information begins to accumulate in your credit report. For this reason, having no credit score can often be just as bad as having a low one. Lenders want to know that you have a history of borrowing money and paying it back on time. After all, if you've never taken out a loan, how can a bank know that you'll pay back its money? So, having nothing on your credit report can result in low credit limits and high interest rates.

With time, though, credit scores can be raised. With every payment, your credit report improves and banks will be more likely to loan you money. These new loans will in turn raise your score even further (as long as you keep making payments, of course).

In general, there are a number of basic steps you can take to raise your credit score. First, ensure that you make payments on time. When payments are past due, that not only has a negative impact on your score, but new creditors will also be reluctant to lend to you while you are delinquent on other accounts.

Being smart about taking on debt is another key factor in keeping your credit score high. As someone who is just starting off in the financial world, you will receive multiple offers to open accounts, say for an introductory credit card or short-term loan. You may also find that as your score increases, you get offers for larger and larger loans. (Predatory lenders are a scourge on the young as well as the old.) But just because banks are offering you those loans doesn't make them a good idea. Instead, you should only take on debt you know you can pay back in a reasonable amount of time.

Lastly, keep an eye on unpaid student loans, medical bills, and parking tickets, all of which can take a negative toll on your credit score. In fact, your credit score will take a major hit from any bill that's sent to a collection agency, so it's in your best interest to avoid letting bills get to that point. Many organizations will agree to keep bills away from collection agencies if you set up a fee-payment system.

18. Which of the following is an opinion stated in the passage?

   A) Credit scores, which range from 300 to 850, are a single value that summarizes an individual's credit history.

   B) Many organizations will agree to keep bills away from collection agencies if you set up a fee-payment system.

   C) After all, if you've never taken out a loan, how can a bank know that you'll pay back its money?

   D) Predatory lenders are a scourge on the young as well as the old.

19. What is the author's primary purpose in writing this essay?

   A) to help readers understand and improve their credit scores

   B) to warn banks about the dangers of lending to people with no credit score

   C) to persuade readers to take out large loans in order to improve their credit scores

   D) to explain to readers how the process of taking out a bank loan works

20. Which statement is not a detail from the passage?

   A) In general, there are a number of basic steps you can take to raise your credit score.

   B) When it comes to credit, everyone begins with a clean slate.

   C) Employers can access your credit score before hiring you.

   D) Predatory lenders are a scourge on the young as well as the old.

21. What is the best summary of this passage?

   A) Individuals with low credit scores will likely have trouble getting credit cards and loans. However, they can improve their credit scores over time.

   B) Having no credit score can often be worse than having a low credit score, so it's important to sign up for credit cards and loans early in life.

   C) Credit scores summarize an individual's credit history and are used by many businesses. They can be improved by making smart financial decisions.

   D) Credit scores can be raised by paying bills on time, taking out reasonably sized loans, and avoiding collection agencies.

22. What can the reader conclude from the passage above?

    A) It is possible to wipe your credit report clean and start over with a blank slate.

    B) A person with a large amount of debt can likely get a loan with a low interest rate because they have demonstrated they are trustworthy.

    C) Someone who has borrowed and paid back large sums of money will get a loan with more favorable terms than someone who has never borrowed money before.

    D) A college student with no credit cards or debt likely has a high credit score.

23. According to the passage, which individual is likely to have the highest credit score?

    A) someone who has had medical bills sent to a collection agency

    B) someone who is in the process of paying back his student loans

    C) someone who has never borrowed any money but pays his bills on time

    D) someone who has borrowed a large amount of money and paid it back on time

24. What is the meaning of the word *distilled* in the first paragraph?

    A) to refine to an essence

    B) to explain at length

    C) to keep records of

    D) to undergo substantial change

HAND WASHING

Hand washing is one of our most powerful weapons against infection. The idea behind hand washing is deceptively simple. Many illnesses are spread when people touch infected surfaces, such as door handles or other people's hands, and then touch their own eyes, mouths, or noses. So, if pathogens can be removed from the hands before they spread, infections can be prevented. When done correctly, hand washing can prevent the spread of many dangerous bacteria and viruses, including those that cause the flu, the common cold, diarrhea, and many acute respiratory illnesses.

The most basic method of hand washing only involves soap and water. Just twenty seconds of scrubbing with soap and a through rinse with water is enough to kill and/or wash away many pathogens. The process doesn't even require warm water—studies have shown that cold water is just as effective at reducing the number of microbes on the hands. While antibacterial soaps are also available, soap and cold water is just as effective.

In recent years, hand sanitizers have become popular as an alternative to hand washing. These gels, liquids, and foams contain a high concentration of alcohol (usually at least sixty percent) which kills most bacteria and fungi; they can also be effective against some, but not all, viruses. There is a downside to hand sanitizer, however. Because the sanitizer isn't rinsed from hands, it only kills pathogens and does nothing to remove organic matter. So, hands "cleaned" with hand sanitizer may still harbor pathogens. Thus, while hand sanitizer can be helpful in situations where soap and clean water isn't available, a simple hand washing is still the best option.

25. Knowing that the temperature of the water does not change the effectiveness of hand washing, it can be concluded that water plays an important role in hand washing because it _____

   a) has antibacterial properties.

   b) physically removes pathogens from hands.

   c) cools hands to make them inhospitable for dangerous bacteria.

   d) is hot enough to kill bacteria.

26. Which of the following is not a fact stated in the passage?

   A) Many infections occur because people get pathogens on their hands and then touch their own eyes, mouths, or noses.

   B) Antibacterial soaps and warm water are the best way to remove pathogens from hands.

   C) Most hand sanitizers have a concentration of at least sixty percent alcohol.

   D) Hand sanitizer can be an acceptable alternative to hand washing when soap and water aren't available.

27. What is the best summary of this passage?

   A) Many diseases are spread by pathogens that can live on the hands. Hand washing is the best way to remove these pathogens and prevent disease.

   B) Simple hand washing can prevent the spread of many common illnesses, including the flu, the common cold, diarrhea, and many acute respiratory illnesses. Hand sanitizer can also kill the pathogens that cause these diseases.

   C) Simple hand washing with soap and cold water is an effective way to reduce the spread of disease. Antibacterial soaps and hand sanitizers may be also be used but are not significantly more effective.

   D) Using hand sanitizer will kill many pathogens, but it will not remove organic matter. Hand washing with soap and water is a better option when it is available.

28. What is the meaning of the word *harbor* in the last paragraph?

   A) to disguise

   B) to hide

   C) to wash away

   D) to give a home

29. What is the author's primary purpose in writing this essay?

   A) to persuade readers of the importance and effectiveness of hand washing with soap and cold water

   B) to dissuade readers from using hand sanitizer

   C) to explain how many common diseases are spread

   D) to describe the many health benefits of hand washing and using hand sanitizer

30. What can the reader conclude from the passage above?

   A) Hand washing would do little to limit infections that spread through particles in the air.

   B) Hand washing is not necessary for people who do not touch their eyes, mouths, or noses with their hands.

   C) Hand sanitizer serves no purpose and should not be used as an alternative to hand washing.

   D) Hand sanitizer will likely soon replace hand washing as the preferred method of removing pathogens from hands.

THE JAZZ AGE

In recent decades, jazz has been associated with New Orleans and festivals like Mardi Gras, but in the 1920s jazz was a booming trend whose influence affected many aspects of American culture. In fact, the years between World War I and the Great Depression were known as the Jazz Age, a term coined by F. Scott Fitzgerald in his famous novel *The Great Gatsby*. Sometimes also called the Roaring Twenties, this time period saw major urban centers experiencing new economic, cultural, and artistic vitality. In the United States, musicians flocked to cities like New York and Chicago, which would became famous hubs for jazz musicians. Ella Fitzgerald, for example, moved from Virginia to New York City to begin her much-lauded singing career, and jazz pioneer Louis Armstrong got his big break in Chicago.

Jazz music was played by and for a more expressive and freed populace than the United States had previously seen. Women had recently gained the right to vote and were publicly drinking and dancing to jazz music. This period marked the emergence of the *flapper*, a woman determined to make a statement about her new role in society. Jazz music also provided the soundtrack for the explosion of African American art and culture now known as the Harlem Renaissance. In addition to Fitzgerald and Armstrong, numerous musicians, including Duke Ellington, Fats Waller, and Bessie Smith, promoted their distinctive and complex music as an integral part of the emerging African American popular culture.

31. What is the main idea of the passage?

   A) People should associate jazz music with the 1920s, not modern New Orleans.

   B) Jazz music played an important role in many cultural movements of the 1920s.

   C) Many famous jazz musicians began their careers in New York City and Chicago.

   D) African Americans were instrumental in launching jazz into mainstream culture.

32. What can the reader conclude from the passage above?

   A) Jazz music was important to minority groups struggling for social equality in the 1920s.

   B) Duke Ellington, Fats Waller, and Bessie Smith were the most important jazz musicians of the Harlem Renaissance.

   C) Women were able to gain the right to vote with the help of jazz musicians.

   D) Duke Ellington, Fats Waller, and Bessie Smith all supported women's right to vote.

33. Which of the following is not a fact stated in the passage?

    A) The years between World War I and the Great Depression were known as the Jazz Age.

    B) Ella Fitzgerald and Louis Armstrong both moved to New York City to start their music careers.

    C) Women danced to jazz music during the 1920s to make a statement about their role in society.

    D) Jazz music was an integral part of the emerging African American popular culture of the 1920s.

34. What can the reader conclude from the passage above?

    A) F. Scott Fitzgerald supported jazz musicians in New York and Chicago.

    B) Jazz music is no longer as popular as it once was.

    C) Both women and African Americans used jazz music as a way of expressing their newfound freedom.

    D) Flappers and African American musicians worked together to produce jazz music.

35. What is the author's primary purpose in writing this essay?

    A) to explain the role jazz musicians played in the Harlem Renaissance

    B) to inform the reader about the many important musicians playing jazz in the 1920s

    C) to discuss how jazz influenced important cultural movements in the 1920s

    D) to provide a history of jazz music in the 20th century

37. The passage is reflective of which of the following types of writing?

    A) technical

    B) expository

    C) persuasive

    D) narrative

36. Which of the following is the topic sentence for the whole passage?

    A) In recent decades, jazz has been associated with New Orleans and festivals like Mardi Gras, but in the 1920s jazz was a booming trend whose influence affected many aspects of American culture.

    B) Sometimes also called the Roaring Twenties, this time period saw major urban cities experiencing new economic, cultural, and artistic vitality.

    C) The Jazz Age brought along with it a more expressive and freed populace.

    D) Jazz music also provided the soundtrack for the explosion of African American art and culture now known as the Harlem Renaissance.

38. *Jazz music also provided the soundtrack for the explosion of African American art and culture now known as the Harlem Renaissance.*

This sentence appears in the second paragraph of the passage. This sentence is best described as which of the following?

    A) theme

    B) topic

    C) main idea

    D) supporting idea

POPCORN

Popcorn is often associated with fun and festivities, both in and out of the home. We eat it in theaters, smothering it in butter, and at home, fresh from the microwave. But popcorn isn't just for fun—it's also a multimillion-dollar industry with a long and fascinating history.

While popcorn might seem like a modern invention, its history actually dates back thousands of years, making it one of the oldest snack foods enjoyed around the world. Popping is believed by food historians to be one of the earliest uses of cultivated corn. In 1948, Herbert Dick and Earle Smith discovered old popcorn dating back 4000 years in the New Mexico Bat Cave. For the Aztecs who called the caves home, popcorn (or *momochitl*) played an important role in society, both as a food staple and in ceremonies. The Aztecs cooked popcorn by heating sand in a fire; when it was heated, kernels were added and would pop when exposed to the heat of the sand.

The American love affair with popcorn began in 1912, when it was first sold in theaters. The popcorn industry flourished during the Great Depression by advertising popcorn as a wholesome and economical food. Selling for five to ten cents a bag, it was a luxury that the downtrodden could afford. With the introduction of mobile popcorn machines at the World's Columbian Exposition, popcorn moved from the theater into fairs and parks. Popcorn continued to rule the snack food kingdom until the rise in popularity of home televisions during the 1950s.

The popcorn industry quickly reacted to its decline in sales by introducing pre-popped and un-popped popcorn for home consumption. However, it wasn't until microwave popcorn became commercially available in 1981 that at-home popcorn consumption began to grow exponentially. With the wide availability of microwaves in the United States, popcorn also began popping up in offices and hotel rooms. The home still remains the most popular popcorn eating spot, though: today, seventy percent of the sixteen billion quarts of popcorn consumed annually in the United States is eaten at home.

39. What can the reader conclude from the passage above?

- **A)** People ate less popcorn in the 1950s than in previous decades because they went to the movies less.
- **B)** Without mobile popcorn machines, people would not have been able to eat popcorn during the Great Depression.
- **C)** People enjoyed popcorn during the Great Depression because it was a luxury food.
- **D)** During the 1800s, people began abandoning theaters to go to fairs and festivals.

40. What is the author's primary purpose in writing this essay?

- **A)** to explain how microwaves affected the popcorn industry
- **B)** to show that popcorn, while popular in American history, is older than many people realize
- **C)** to illustrate the global history of popcorn from ancient cultures to modern times
- **D)** to demonstrate the importance of popcorn in various cultures

Answer Key

1.	A)	21.	C)
2.	C)	22.	C)
3.	D)	23.	D)
4.	C)	24.	A)
5.	A)	25.	B)
6.	A)	26.	B)
7.	A)	27.	C)
8.	B)	28.	D)
9.	D)	29.	A)
10.	C)	30.	A)
11.	A)	31.	B)
12.	C)	32.	A)
13.	A)	33.	B)
14.	A)	34.	C)
15.	B)	35.	C)
16.	B)	36.	B)
17.	A)	37.	A)
18.	D)	38.	C)
19.	A)	39.	A)
20.	C)	40.	B)

LANGUAGE

NOUNS AND PRONOUNS

NOUNS are people, places, or things. The subject of a sentence is typically a noun. For example, in the sentence *The hospital was very clean*, the subject, *hospital*, is a noun; it is a place. **PRONOUNS** stand in for nouns and can be used to make sentences sound less repetitive. Take the sentence, "Sam stayed home from school because Sam was not feeling well." The word *Sam* appears twice in the same sentence. Instead, you can use the pronoun *he* to stand in for *Sam* and say, "Sam stayed home from school because he was not feeling well."

Singular Pronouns
- I, me, my, mine
- you, your, yours
- he, him, his
- she, her, hers
- it, its

Plural Pronouns
- we, us, our, ours
- they, them, their, theirs

Because pronouns take the place of nouns, they need to agree both in number and gender with the noun they replace. So, a plural noun needs a plural pronoun, and a noun referring to something feminine needs a feminine pronoun. In the first sentence in this paragraph, for example, the plural pronoun *they* replaced the plural noun *pronouns*. There will usually be several questions on the English and Language Usage section that cover pronoun agreement, so it's good to get comfortable spotting pronouns.

> Wrong: If a student forgets their homework, they will not receive a grade.
>
> Correct: If a student forgets his or her homework, he or she will not receive a grade.

Student is a singular noun, but *their* and *they* are plural pronouns. So, the first sentence is incorrect. To correct it, use the singular pronoun *his* or *her*, or *he* or *she*.

> Wrong: Everybody will receive their paychecks promptly.
>
> Correct: Everybody will receive his or her paycheck promptly.

Everybody is a singular noun, but *their* is a plural pronoun. So, this sentence is incorrect. To correct it, use the singular pronoun *his* or *her*.

> Wrong: When nurses scrub in to surgery, you should wash your hands.
>
> Correct: When nurses scrub in to surgery, they should wash their hands.

This sentence begins in third-person perspective and then switches to second-person perspective. So, this sentence is incorrect. To correct it, use a third-person pronoun in the second clause.

> Wrong: After the teacher spoke to the student, she realized her mistake.
>
> Correct: After Mr. White spoke to his student, she realized her mistake.
> (*She* and *her* refer to the student.)
>
> Correct: After speaking to the student, the teacher realized her own mistake.
> (*Her* refers to the teacher.)

This sentence refers to a teacher and a student. But whom does *she* refer to, the teacher or the student? To eliminate the ambiguity, use specific names or state more specifically who made the mistake.

Examples

I have lived in Minnesota since August, but I still don't own a warm coat or gloves.

1. Which of the following lists includes all the nouns in the sentence?

    A) coat, gloves

    B) I, coat, gloves

    C) Minnesota, August, coat, gloves

    D) I, Minnesota, August, warm, coat, gloves

    Answer:

    C) is correct. *Minnesota* and *August* are proper nouns, and *coat* and *gloves* are common nouns. *I* is a pronoun, and *warm* is an adjective that modifies *coat*.

2. In which of the following sentences do the nouns and pronouns NOT agree?

    A) After we walked inside, we took off our hats and shoes and hung them in the closet.

    B) The members of the band should leave her instruments in the rehearsal room.

    C) The janitor on duty should rinse out his or her mop before leaving for the day.

    D) When you see someone in trouble, you should always try to help them.

    Answer:

    B) is correct. *The members of the band* is plural, so it should be replaced by the plural pronoun *their* instead of the singular *her*.

VERBS

A **VERB** is the action of a sentence: it describes what the subject of the sentence is or is doing. Verbs must match the subject of the sentence in person and number, and must be in the proper tense—past, present, or future.

Person describes the relationship of the speaker to the subject of the sentence: first (I, we), second (you), and third (he, she, it, they). *Number* refers to whether the subject of the sentence is singular or plural. Verbs are conjugated to match the person and number of the subject.

Table 2.1. Conjugating Verbs for Person

PERSON	SINGULAR	PLURAL
First	I jump	we jump
Second	you jump	you jump
Third	he/she/it jumps	they jump

> Wrong: The cat chase the ball while the dogs runs in the yard.
>
> Correct: The cat chases the ball while the dogs run in the yard.

Cat is singular, so it takes a singular verb (which confusingly ends with an *s*); *dogs* is plural, so it needs a plural verb.

> Wrong: The cars that had been recalled by the manufacturer was returned within a few months.
>
> Correct: The cars that had been recalled by the manufacturer were returned within a few months.

Sometimes, the subject and verb are separated by clauses or phrases. Here, the subject *cars* is separated from the verb by the relatively long phrase "that had been recalled by the manufacturer," making it more difficult to determine how to correctly conjugate the verb.

> Correct: The doctor and nurse work in the hospital.
>
> Correct: Neither the nurse nor her boss was scheduled to take a vacation.
>
> Correct: Either the patient or her parents need to sign the release forms.

When the subject contains two or more nouns connected by *and*, that subject becomes plural and requires a plural verb. Singular subjects joined by *either/or*, *neither/nor*, or *not only/but also* remain singular; when these words join plural and singular subjects, the verb should match the closest subject.

Finally, verbs must be conjugated for tense, which shows when the action happened. Some conjugations include helping verbs like *was*, *have*, *have been*, and *will have been*.

> ⚠ If the subject is separated from the verb, cross out the phrases between them to make conjugation easier.

Table 2.2. Verb Tenses

TENSE	PAST	PRESENT	FUTURE
Simple	I <u>gave</u> her a gift yesterday.	I <u>give</u> her a gift every day.	I <u>will give</u> her a gift on her birthday.
Continuous	I <u>was giving</u> her a gift when you got here.	I <u>am giving</u> her a gift; come in!	I <u>will be giving</u> her a gift at dinner.
Perfect	I <u>had given</u> her a gift before you got there.	I <u>have given</u> her a gift already.	I <u>will have given</u> her a gift by midnight.
Perfect continuous	Her friends <u>had been giving</u> her gifts all night when I arrived.	I <u>have been giving</u> her gifts every year for nine years.	I <u>will have been giving</u> her gifts on holidays for ten years next year.

Tense must also be consistent throughout the sentence and the passage. For example, the sentence *I was baking cookies and eat some dough* sounds strange. That is because the two verbs, *was baking* and *eat*, are in different tenses. *Was baking* occurred in the past; *eat*, on the other hand, occurs in the present. To make them consistent, change *eat* to *ate*.

> Wrong: Because it will rain during the party last night, we had to move the tables inside.
>
> Correct: Because it rained during the party last night, we had to move the tables inside.

All the verb tenses in a sentence need to agree both with each other and with the other information in the sentence. In the first sentence above, the tense does not match the other information in the sentence: *last night* indicates the past (*rained*), not the future (*will rain*).

Examples

1. Which of the following sentences contains an incorrectly conjugated verb?
   - **A)** The brother and sister runs very fast.
   - **B)** Neither Anne nor Suzy likes the soup.
   - **C)** The mother and father love their new baby.
   - **D)** Either Jack or Jill will pick up the pizza.

   Answer:

   A) is correct. Choice A should read "The brother and sister run very fast." When the subject contains two or more nouns connected by *and*, the subject is plural and requires a plural verb.

2. Which of the following sentences contains an incorrect verb tense?
   - **A)** After the show ended, we drove to the restaurant for dinner.
   - **B)** Anne went to the mall before she headed home.
   - **C)** Johnny went to the movies after he cleans the kitchen.
   - **D)** Before the alarm sounded, smoke filled the cafeteria.

   Answer:

   C) is correct. Choice C should read "Johnny will go to the movies after he cleans the kitchen." It does not make sense to say that Johnny does something in the past (*went to the movies*) after doing something in the present (*after he cleans*).

ADJECTIVES AND ADVERBS

ADJECTIVES provide more information about a noun in a sentence. Take the sentence, "The boy hit the ball." If you want your readers to know more about the noun *boy*, you could use an adjective to describe him: *the little boy, the young boy, the tall boy*.

ADVERBS and adjectives are similar because they provide more information about a part of a sentence. However, adverbs do not describe nouns—that's an adjective's job. Instead, adverbs describe verbs, adjectives, and even other adverbs. For example, in the sentence "The doctor had recently hired a new employee," the adverb *recently* tells us more about how the action *hired* took place.

Adjectives, adverbs, and MODIFYING PHRASES (groups of words that together modify another word) should be placed as close as possible to the word they modify. Separating words from their modifiers can create incorrect or confusing sentences.

> Wrong: Running through the hall, the bell rang and the student knew she was late.
>
> Correct: Running through the hall, the student heard the bell ring and knew she was late.

The phrase *running through the hall* should be placed next to *student*, the noun it modifies.

The suffixes *–er* and *–est* are often used to modify adjectives when a sentence is making a comparison. The suffix *–er* is used when comparing two things, and the suffix *–est* is used when comparing more than two.

> Anne is taller than Steve, but Steve is more coordinated.
>
> Of the five brothers, Billy is the funniest, and Alex is the most intelligent.

Adjectives longer than two syllables are compared using *more* (for two things) or *most* (for three or more things).

> Wrong: Of my two friends, Clara is the smartest.
>
> Correct: Of my two friends, Clara is smarter.

More and *most* should not be used in conjunction with *–er* and *–est* endings.

> Wrong: My most warmest sweater is made of wool.
>
> Correct: My warmest sweater is made of wool.

Examples

The new chef carefully stirred the boiling soup and then lowered the heat.

1. Which of the following lists includes all the adjectives in the sentence?

   A) new, boiling

   B) new, carefully, boiling

   C) new, carefully, boiling, heat

   D) new, carefully, boiling, lowered, heat

   Answer:

   A) is correct. *New* modifies the noun *chef*, and *boiling* modifies the noun *soup*. *Carefully* is an adverb modifying the verb *stirred*. *Lowered* is a verb, and *heat* is a noun.

2. Which of the following sentences contains an adjective error?

   A) The new red car was faster than the old blue car.

   B) Reggie's apartment is in the tallest building on the block.

   C) The slice of cake was tastier than the brownie.

   D) Of the four speeches, Jerry's was the most long.

PHRASES

To understand what a phrase is, you have to know about subjects and predicates. The SUBJECT is what the sentence is about; the PREDICATE contains the verb and its modifiers.

> The nurse at the front desk will answer any questions you have.

The subject is *the nurse at the front desk*, and the predicate is *will answer any questions you have*.

A PHRASE is a group of words that communicates only part of an idea because it lacks either a subject or a predicate. Phrases are categorized based on the main word in the phrase. A PREPOSITIONAL PHRASE begins with a preposition and ends with an object of the preposition, a VERB PHRASE is composed of the main verb along with any helping verbs, and a NOUN PHRASE consists of a noun and its modifiers.

> Prepositional phrase: The dog is hiding <u>under the porch</u>.
>
> Verb phrase: The chef <u>wanted to cook</u> a different dish.
>
> Noun phrase: <u>The big red barn</u> rests beside <u>the vacant chicken house</u>.

Example

Identify the type of phrase underlined in the following sentence.

David, <u>smelling the fresh bread baking,</u> smiled as he entered the kitchen.

A) prepositional phrase

B) noun phrase

C) verb phrase

D) verbal phrase

Answer:

D) is correct. The phrase is a verbal phrase modifying the noun *David*. It begins with the word *smelling*, derived from the verb *to smell*.

CLAUSES

CLAUSES contain both a subject and a predicate. They can be either independent or dependent. An INDEPENDENT (or main) CLAUSE can stand alone as its own sentence.

> The dog ate her homework.

Dependent (or subordinate) clauses cannot stand alone as their own sentences. They start with a subordinating conjunction, relative pronoun, or relative adjective, which will make them sound incomplete.

> Because the dog ate her homework

A sentence can be classified as simple, compound, complex, or compound-complex based on the type and number of clauses it has.

Table 2.3. Types of Clauses

SENTENCE TYPE	NUMBER OF INDEPENDENT CLAUSES	NUMBER OF DEPENDENT CLAUSES
simple	1	0
compound	2 or more	0
complex	1	1 or more
compound-complex	2 or more	1 or more

A **SIMPLE SENTENCE** consists of one independent clause. Because there are no dependent clauses in a simple sentence, it can be a two-word sentence, with one word being the subject and the other word being the verb, such as *I ran*. However, a simple sentence can also contain prepositions, adjectives, and adverbs. Even though these additions can extend the length of a simple sentence, it is still considered a simple sentence as long as it does not contain any dependent clauses.

> Simple: San Francisco in the springtime is one of my favorite places to visit.

Although the sentence is lengthy, it is simple because it contains only one subject and one verb (*San Francisco* and *is*), modified by additional phrases.

COMPOUND SENTENCES have two or more independent clauses and no dependent clauses. Usually a comma and a coordinating conjunction (the FANBOYS: For, And, Nor, But, Or, Yet, and So) join the independent clauses, though semicolons can be used as well.

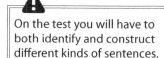

On the test you will have to both identify and construct different kinds of sentences.

> Compound: The game was canceled, but we will still practice on Saturday.

This sentence is made up of two independent clauses joined by a conjunction (*but*), so it is compound.

COMPLEX SENTENCES have one independent clause and at least one dependent clause. The two clauses will be joined by a subordinating conjunction.

> Complex: I love listening to the radio in the car because I can sing along.

The sentence has one independent clause (*I love...car*) and one dependent (*because I... along*), so it is complex.

COMPOUND-COMPLEX SENTENCES have two or more independent clauses and at least one dependent clause. Compound-complex sentences will have both a coordinating and a subordinating conjunction.

> I wanted to get a dog, but I have a fish because my roommate is allergic to pet dander.

This sentence has three clauses: two independent (*I wanted...dog* and *I have a fish*) and one dependent (*because my...dander*), so it is compound-complex.

Examples

1. Which of the following choices is a simple sentence?

   A) Elsa drove while Erica navigated.

   B) Betty ordered a fruit salad, and Sue ordered eggs.

   C) Because she was late, Jenny ran down the hall.

   D) John ate breakfast with his mother, brother, and father.

   Answer:

   D) is correct. Choice D contains one independent clause with one subject and one verb. Choices A and C are complex sentences because they each contain both a dependent and independent clause. Choice B contains two independent clauses joined by a conjunction and is therefore a compound sentence.

2. Which of the following sentences is a compound-complex sentence?

   A) While they were at the game, Anne cheered for the home team, but Harvey rooted for the underdogs.

   B) The rain flooded all of the driveway, some of the yard, and even part of the sidewalk across the street.

   C) After everyone finished the test, Mr. Brown passed a bowl of candy around the classroom.

   D) All the flowers in the front yard are in bloom, and the trees around the house are lush and green.

   Answer:

   A) is correct. Choice A is a compound-complex sentence because it contains two independent clauses and one dependent clause. Despite its length, choice B is a simple sentence because it contains only one independent clause. Choice C is a complex sentence because it contains one dependent clause and one independent clause. Choice D is a compound sentence; it contains two independent clauses.

TEST YOUR KNOWLEDGE

Questions 1 – 5 are based on the following original passage. Sentences are numbered at the end for easy reference within the questions.

Examining the impact my lifestyle has on the earth's resources is, I believe, a fascinating and valuable thing to do (1). According to the Earth Day Network ecological footprint calculator, it would take four planet earths to sustain the human population if everyone used as many resources as I do (2). My "ecological footprint," or the amount of productive area of the earth that is required to produce the resources I consume, is therefore larger than the footprints of most of the population (3). It is hard to balance the luxuries and opportunities I have available to me with doing what I know to be better from an ecological standpoint (4).

It is fairly easy for me to recycle, so I do it, but it would be much harder to forgo the opportunity to travel by plane or eat my favorite fruits that have been flown to the supermarket from a different country (5). Although I get ecological points for my recycling habits, my use of public transportation, and living in an apartment complex rather than a free-standing residence, <u>my footprint expands when it is taken into account my not-entirely-local diet</u>, my occasional use of a car, my three magazine subscriptions, and my history of flying more than ten hours a year (6). I feel that realizing just how unfair my share of the earth's resources have been should help me to change at least some of my bad habits (7).

1. Which of the following shows the best version of sentence 1?
   A) It is fascinating and valuable to examine the impact that my lifestyle has on the earth's resources.
   B) Examining the impact my lifestyle has on the earth's resources is a fascinating and valuable thing to do.
   C) To examine the impact my lifestyle has on the earth's resources is fascinating and is also valuable.
   D) The impact of my lifestyle on the earth's resources is fascinating and valuable to examine.
   E) Examining the impact my lifestyle has on the earth's resources is, I believe, a fascinating and valuable thing to do.

2. Sentence 4 would best fit if it were moved where in this composition?
   A) 2.
   B) After sentence 5.
   C) After sentence 6.
   D) At the end of paragraph 2.
   E) Sentence 4 is best left where it is.

3. Which two sentences would be improved by switching positions?
   A) 1 and 2.
   B) 2 and 7.
   C) 3 and 4.
   D) 5 and 6.
   E) 6 and 7.

4. How could sentences 2 and 3 best be combined?

   A) According to the Earth Day Network ecological footprint calculator, it would take four planet earths to sustain the human population if everyone used as many resources as I do because I have a very large "ecological footprint," which is the amount of productive area of the earth that is required to produce the resources I consume.

   B) According to the Earth Day Network ecological footprint calculator, which calculates the amount of productive area of the earth that is required to produce the resources one consumes, it would take four planet earths to sustain the human population if everyone had a footprint as large as mine.

   C) According to the Earth Day Network ecological footprint calculator, it would take four planet earths to sustain the human population if everyone used as many resources as I do; my "ecological footprint," or the amount of productive area of the earth that is required to produce the resources I consume, is therefore larger than the footprints of most of the population.

   D) According to the Earth Day Network ecological footprint calculator, which measures the amount of productive area of the earth that is required to produce the resources a person consumes, my footprint is larger than that of most; it would take four planet earths to sustain the human population if everyone consumed as much as I do.

   E) According to the Earth Day Network ecological footprint calculator, my "ecological footprint," or the amount of productive area of the earth that is required to produce the resources I consume, would require four planet earths if it were to be the footprint of the human population; it is therefore larger than the footprints of most of the population.

5. How could the underlined part of sentence 6 best be rewritten?

   A) "my footprint expands when taken into account my not-entirely-local diet"

   B) "my footprint expands when taken into account are my not-entirely-local diet"

   C) "my footprint expands when we take into account my not-entirely-local diet"

   D) "my footprint expands when one takes into account my not-entirely-local diet"

   E) "my footprint expands when it is taken into account my not-entirely-local diet"

6. Which revision would most improve sentence 7?

   A) Eliminate the phrase "I feel that."

   B) Change "should help me" to "will help me."

   C) Add the phrase "In conclusion," to the beginning.

   D) Change "have been" to "has been."

   E) Eliminate the phrase "at least some of."

Questions 7 – 12 are based on the short passage below, which is excerpted from Thomas Huxley's preface to his Collected Essays: Volume V *(public domain) and modified slightly. Sentences are numbered at the end for easy reference within the questions.*

I had set out on a journey, with no other purpose than that of exploring a certain province of natural knowledge, I strayed no hair's breadth from the course which it was my right and my duty to pursue; and yet I found that, whatever route I took, before long, I came to a tall and formidable-looking fence (1). Confident I might be in the existence of an ancient and indefeasible right of way, before me stood the thorny barrier with its comminatory notice-board—"No Thoroughfare. By order" (2). There seemed no way over; nor did the prospect of creeping round, as I saw some do, attracts me (3). True there was no longer any cause to fear the spring guns and man-traps set by former lords of the manor; but one is apt to get very dirty going on all-fours (4). The only alternatives were either to give up my journey—which I was not minded to do—or to break the fence down and go through it (5). I swiftly ruled out crawling under as an option (6). I also ruled out turning back (7).

7. How could sentence 1 best be changed?
   A) The comma after journey should be removed.
   B) The comma after knowledge should be changed to a semicolon.
   C) "and yet" should be eliminated.
   D) Change "I had set out" to "I set out."
   E) No change.

8. Sentence 6 should be placed where in the passage?
   A) After sentence 1.
   B) After sentence 2.
   C) After sentence 3.
   D) After sentence 4.
   E) Left after sentence 5.

9. Which edit should be made in sentence 3?
   A) "nor" should be changed to "or."
   B) "seemed" should be changed to "seems."
   C) "me" should be changed to "I."
   D) "attracts" should be changed to "attract."
   E) No edit should be made.

10. How could sentences 6 and 7 best be combined?
    A) Swiftly, I ruled out crawling under as an option and also turning back.
    B) Ruling out two options swiftly: crawling under and turning back.
    C) I swiftly ruled out the options of crawling under or turning back.
    D) I ruled out crawling under as an option and I swiftly also ruled out turning back.
    E) I swiftly ruled out crawling under as an option and also turning back.

11. Which word could be inserted at the beginning of sentence 2 before "confident" to best clarify the meaning?
    A) Even.
    B) However.
    C) Hardly.
    D) Finally.
    E) Especially.

12. Which of the following is the best way to split sentence 1 into two separate sentences?

- **A)** I had set out on a journey, with no other purpose than that of exploring a certain province of natural knowledge. I strayed no hair's breadth from the course which it was my right and my duty to pursue; and yet I found that, whatever route I took, before long, I came to a tall and formidable-looking fence.

- **B)** I had set out on a journey, with no other purpose than that of exploring a certain province of natural knowledge, I strayed no hair's breadth from the course which it was my right and my duty to pursue. Yet I found that, whatever route I took, before long, I came to a tall and formidable-looking fence.

- **C)** I had set out on a journey, with no other purpose than that of exploring a certain province of natural knowledge, I strayed no hair's breadth from the course which it was my right and my duty to pursue; and yet I found that, whatever route I took, before long. I came to a tall and formidable-looking fence.

- **D)** I had set out on a journey. With no other purpose than that of exploring a certain province of natural knowledge, I strayed no hair's breadth from the course which it was my right and my duty to pursue; and yet I found that, whatever route I took, before long, I came to a tall and formidable-looking fence.

- **E)** I had set out on a journey, with no other purpose than that of exploring a certain province of natural knowledge, I strayed no hair's breadth from the course which it was my right and my duty to pursue; and yet. I found that, whatever route I took, before long, I came to a tall and formidable-looking fence.

Questions 13 – 16 are based on the passage below.

Who doesn't love a good cat meme? (1) It turns out that cats are more popular around the world than anyone had realized; with the proliferation of YouTube and social media, cats have taken the internet by storm. (2) From Grumpy Cat to Waffles, from the United States to Japan, cats appear in funny pictures, hilarious videos, and have even gone on to make their owners millions of dollars. (3)

Until recently, it had been believed that dogs were the most popular pet in the United States, with cats lagging behind in second place. (4) Dogs, "man's best friend," can be trained to do certain tricks and tasks, can be fun workout companions who play Frisbee and fetch with their owners, and can even help protect property. (5) While cats may have their uses in pest control, they are often reluctant to work on command, and very few are willing to submit to the humiliation of a collar and leash for a walk outside. (6) Still, it turns out that their funny antics and remarkable athletic prowess, even indoors, make for good TV.

(7) And so the internet is filled with cats large and small, lean and fat, wearing pieces of bread, making playthings out of boxes, jumping to amazing heights, and just looking hilariously grumpy. (8) Cats of internet fame now appear at conventions and festivals around the world, and people wait in line for hours just for a glimpse at their favorite feline celebrity. (9)

13. What would be a good title for this essay, keeping in mind both the topic and the tone?

- **A)** The Rise and Fall of Famous Felines: From Grumpy Cat to Smushyface
- **B)** Dog versus Cat: the Battle Continues, from the Internet to the Convention Center
- **C)** Felines Online! Pet Popularity, Feline Fame, and the Internet Age
- **D)** Cats for Cash: is Feline Fame Really Catsploitation?

14. Which sentence best completes the first paragraph in order to create a good transition between two paragraphs?

    A)   But cats have not always been in the spotlight; in fact, they had been relegated to a secondary position in the known hierarchy of pet popularity in popular culture.

    B)   Indeed, cats are taking the world by storm.

    C)   Cats are by far the most popular pet in the world, and cat ownership continues to rise.

    D)   Thanks to the internet, cat marketability is becoming a field requiring true expertise, and there are even entrepreneurs who specialize in representing felines and their owners in public relations.

15. Which revision more concisely revises sentences (6) and (7)?

    A)   No change

    B)   On the other hand, cats are useful for pest control, they are often reluctant to work on command, and very few are willing to submit to the humiliation of a collar and leash for a walk outside. (6) However, it turns out that their funny antics and remarkable athletic prowess, even indoors, make for good TV. (7)

    C)   Cats are useful for pest control, but they are often reluctant to work on command; moreover, very few are willing to submit to the humiliation of a collar and leash for a walk outside. (6) But it turns out that cats are more interesting—and funnier—than anyone realized, and their antics make for good TV. (7)

    D)   Cats are funnier and more interesting than dogs, but are only good for pest control—they won't go for walks on leashes or learn commands.

16. What would be the best sentence to follow sentence 9, in keeping with the theme of the entire paragraph?

    A)   Some dog owners are getting in on the act too, filming their dogs doing funny things and putting them on YouTube, but they don't get nearly as many hits as the cats do…at least not yet.

    B)   Some of the cat owners have become quite media-savvy, and their cats now grace everything from coffee mugs to key chains to t-shirts; while waiting in line, fans are often enticed to buy these trinkets, but this irritates some fans.

    C)   Some commentators believe that the cat owners are exploiting their cats, who no doubt would prefer to be at home napping in the sun or chasing mice.

    D)   We mourn internet sensations like Chairman Meow who have passed on, and laud newcomers like Smushyface who have risen to the challenge of feline fame.

Questions 17 – 20 are based on the passage below.

It sometimes seems like controversy over social media is never-ending. (1) Social media helps keep friends and family members in touch, helps transmit important news, from weather alerts to updates from warzones, out to the community and to the world, and provides opportunities for businesses to promote their products and reach new customers. (2) However, it also puts vulnerable people at risk, especially teenagers. (3) Cyber-bullying is on the rise, with sad stories of teenage depression and even suicide as a result of it appearing in the news. (4)

Vulnerable people can connect with people in similar difficult circumstances through Facebook groups, online forums, and other sources to find support. (5) Anonymous meeting points are especially helpful for people who are in recovery from mental illnesses like depression or eating disorders; they can confide in other people who have suffered from the same diseases and find the support they need. (6) Not everyone has access to counseling or the ◼ means to afford it; perhaps some forms of social media could be a stopgap solution for those in need. (7) Still, there is always the risk of "trolls," people who join these groups only to bully and shame people who really need help. (8)

17. Which sentence best completes the first paragraph in order to create a good transition between two paragraphs?

   A) Social media might do more harm than good in a cruel, unpredictable world; the anonymous world of the internet only brings out the worst in people, and we all must do our part to protect the most vulnerable.

   B) Many people argue that despite its uses, some restrictions should be placed on social media, especially the larger, more influential outlets like Facebook and Twitter.

   C) It might be said that social media is a two-edged sword, something that can enable supportive interaction but also risk facilitating hurtful, abusive behavior.

   D) The tragic stories of cyber-bullying only show that age limits should be placed on social media and even internet use; clearly, teenagers are unable to make good decisions when it comes to social situations, and the anonymity of the internet only enables abusive behavior.

18. What would be the best way to rewrite sentence 5?

   A) No change

   B) Many people who suffer from mental illnesses are isolated and vulnerable to cyber-bullying; social media can provide forums where they can find support from others in similar positions.

   C) It is hard for people who struggle with cyber-bullying because they might also suffer from mental illnesses and therefore feel very alone. With social media, they can connect with other people who also suffer from mental illnesses and form online support groups.

   D) Thanks to the anonymity of the internet, people can stay anonymous and still use social media to connect with other people and find support so they don't feel so alone.

19. What sentence would best follow sentence 8?

   A) Unfortunately the internet is plagued by trolls; finding respite from bullies online even in safe zones set up for the vulnerable is nearly impossible, so members of such groups or sites must remain vigilant and enforce rules about what constitutes abusive behavior.

   B) Fortunately, in these supportive environments, the bullied can become bullies themselves and drive the trolls away – a fate they deserve.

   C) No one is sure how the word *trolls* came to describe online bullies, but it is surely a title they deserve; hiding behind anonymity in order to hurt other people's feelings is nothing to be proud of.

   D) Thanks to online moderators, people may only join supportive online communities after a rigorous screening process, including background checks.

20. Some people feel very isolated or ashamed of mental illnesses or emotional conditions, to the point where they are not comfortable seeking out help, or do not know where to turn to get it; fears of criticism, being thought of as "crazy", losing friends, jobs, and other stigma may prevent them from pursuing therapy or treatment.

Where would the sentence above best be placed in the draft essay?

A) after sentence 3

B) after sentence 7

C) before sentence 5

D) after sentence 5

Questions 21 – 24 are based on the passage below.

To stay or not to stay? (1) That is the question that faces many high school students as they consider colleges. (2) Whether to attend a college far from home depends on a variety of factors, from cost to personal preference, from opportunities at home to connections around the country or even around the world. (3)

Cost and family are two important factors. One student from Louisiana won a full scholarship to a school in California. (4) So even though she was admitted to several nearby schools in her home state, it was cheaper for her to move across the country, even though she would be far from her family. (5) Another student chose to stay home in Wisconsin and attend a state school for a year in order to save money on tuition and room and board; following his freshman year, he was able to apply to his out-of-state dream school in Chicago and could afford three years away from home. (6)

21. Which sentence best starts the second paragraph in order to create a good transition between two paragraphs?

A) A recent study of several students across the nation revealed some of the reasons students chose to leave home or stay there for their college years.

B) The sheer size of the United States provides limitless opportunities for young people seeking a university education; fifty states and six time zones gives students – even those without passports – a lot of options.

C) Some states, like Texas and California, are so big in terms of geographic size and population that it is possible for a student to attend a great school without even leaving his or her home state.

D) It can be hard for many students to leave their home region because of the many cultural differences found across our country, but it is a great learning experience for young people in the long term.

22. What would be the best example to use to develop the second paragraph?

A) a student who travels from Florida to South America to learn Spanish for a year before attending university in Texas, in order to better prepare to major in Latin American studies

B) a student from North Carolina who chooses to study in Arizona because her aunt and uncle live there; she is familiar with the state and can live with them for her first year of college

C) a student from Maine who is considering college but plans to join the military after high school

D) a student who wins a sports scholarship and so attends a university to play on its football team

23. What would be a good way to open a third paragraph of this essay?

   A) Surely, it is important for students to follow their dreams, even if they must ignore their families' wishes and go to college in another state.

   B) Other factors students took into account were their academic and professional interests, seeking out schools that specialized in their chosen career paths or that had the best facilities and professors in their fields.

   C) Some students were willing to stay at home and work, even if it meant waiting a year or two to begin their studies.

   D) A tiny minority of students believed it was more important to get married and have children than to go to college, but only a few respondents reported this belief.

24. So even though she was admitted to several nearby schools in her home state, it was cheaper for her to move across the country, even though she would be far from her family. (5)

   What would be the best way to rewrite the sentence above?

   A) Even though she had a lot of opportunities in her home state because she could go to college there and live with her family, she went across the country because it was cheaper, since she had a scholarship.

   B) It was cheaper for her to move across the country, even though she was admitted to several nearby schools, and even though she would be far from home.

   C) Despite being accepted to several nearby schools, it was cheaper for her to move across the country.

   D) Despite her acceptance to several nearby schools, it was cheaper for her to move across the country.

Questions 25 – 28 are based on the passage below.

Americans continue to debate the merits of legalizing drugs. (1) Although many states have decriminalized the possession of marijuana, and some have outright legalized it altogether, still others retain harsh penalties for its consumption. (2) There are no easy answers here. (3)

   In some states, citizens have agreed on a policy of allowing the use of marijuana for therapeutic purposes. (4) Medical marijuana is used to treat a variety of ailments, and can be obtained with a prescription. (5) It has helped many people suffering from serious afflictions, like cancer, with chronic pain and other conditions. (6) More research must be done in order to uncover any other uses for the drug in medicine. (7) Still, detractors from medical marijuana fear that any level of legal tolerance for the drug is unsafe. (8) Their fears are not entirely unfounded. (9) There is ample evidence to suggest that people who struggle with drug addiction began by abusing marijuana. (10) This may not be a risk for all users, though. (11)

25. Which sentence would best open the second paragraph?

   A) One compromise has been to legalize marijuana for use in medicine and healing.

   B) Some doctors believe in medical marijuana.

   C) It has been proven that in small doses, marijuana can be medically beneficial.

   D) Not all Americans believe that marijuana should be legal for medical uses, but it is still used in medicine in some states.

26. Which sentence best replaces sentence 3 in order to provide more clarity and better transition between the two paragraphs?

   A) For many states, a solution lies somewhere in the middle.

   B) Legalizing the use of marijuana for some purposes has been a solution agreed upon in a number of states.

   C) Several states have found consensus by legalizing marijuana for a limited number of uses.

   D) For sure, outright legalization is not the solution at the federal level.

27. More research must be done in order to uncover any other uses for the drug in medicine. (7)

   What is the best way to rewrite the sentence above?

   A) However, more research must be done in order to determine whether there are further therapeutic uses for marijuana.

   B) In this case, it is clear that no further research is needed as to the efficacy of medical marijuana, and research would be better spent on cures to these diseases.

   C) It is possible that it may have other uses in medicine as well; further research may lead to more information.

   D) Without further research, there would be no need to prescribe medical marijuana.

Questions 28-40 are based on the passage below.

Traveling on commercial airlines has changed substantially <u>over years</u>. (1) When commercial air travel first became available, it was so expensive that usually only businessmen could afford <u>to do so</u>. (2) Airplane efficiency, the relative cost of fossil fuels, <u>and using economies</u> of scale have all contributed to make travel by air more affordable and common. (3) These days, there are nearly 30,000 commercial air flights in the world each day! (4)

Depending on the size of the airport you are departing from, you should arrive 90 minutes to two and a half hours before your plane leaves. (5) Things like checking your luggage and flying internationally can make the process of getting to your gate take longer. (6) If you fly out of a very busy airport, like <u>LaGuardia, in</u> New York City, on a very busy travel day, like the day before Thanksgiving, you can easily miss your flight if you don't arrive early enough. (7)

Security processes for passengers have also changed. (8) In the 1960s, there was <u>hardly any</u> security: you could just buy your ticket and walk on to the plane the day of the flight without even needing to show identification. (9) In the 1970s, American commercial airlines started installing sky marshals on many <u>flights, an</u> undercover law enforcement officers who would protect the passengers from a potential hijacking. (10)

Also in the early 1970s, the federal government began to require that airlines screen passengers and their luggage for things like weapons and bombs. (11) After the 2001 terrorist attacks in the United States, these requirements were <u>stringently enforced</u>. (12) Family members can no longer meet someone at the gate<u>; only ticketed passengers are allowed into the gate area</u>. (13) The definition of <u>weapons are</u> not allowed is expanded every time there is a new incident for example liquids are now restricted on planes after an attempted planned attack using gel explosives in 2006. (14)

Despite the hassles of traveling by air, it is still a boon to modern <u>life. (15) Still, some</u> businesses are moving away from sending employees on airplane trips, <u>as</u> face-to-face video conferencing technologies improve. (16) A trip which might take ten hours by car <u>can take only</u> two hours by plane. (17) However, the ability to travel quickly by air <u>will always be valued, by citizens</u> of our modern society. (18)

28. Which of the following is the best change to the underlined portion of sentence 1?

A) No Change.

B) "over the years"

C) "over time"

D) Delete.

29. Which of the following is the best change to the underlined portion of sentence 2?

A) No Change.

B) "to do it"

C) "to fly"

D) "do so"

30. Which of the following is the best change to the underlined portion of sentence 3?

A) No Change.

B) "using economies"

C) "and the use of economies"

D) "and economies"

31. Which of the following is the best change to the underlined portion of sentence 7?

A) No Change.

B) "La Guardia in"

C) "La Guardia; in"

D) "La Guardia,"

32. Which of the following is the best change to the underlined portion of sentence 9?

A) No Change.

B) "hardly"

C) "no"

D) "barely"

33. Which of the following is the best change to the underlined portion of sentence 10?

A) No Change.

B) "flights; an"

C) "flights. Marshals are"

D) "flights, marshals are"

34. Which of the following is the best change to the underlined portion of sentence 12?
    A) No Change.
    B) "stiffly upheld"
    C) "enforced with more stringency"
    D) "more stringently enforced"

35. If the underlined portion in sentence 13 were deleted, the passage would lose:
    A) No Change.
    B) An explanation of the screening process.
    C) Ambiguity over why family members are no longer allowed at the gate.
    D) A further specific example of how regulations have changed over time.

36. Which of the following is the best change to the underlined portion in sentence 14?
    A) No Change.
    B) "weapon is"
    C) "weapons"
    D) "weapons which are"

37. Which of the following is the proper transition between sentences 15 & 16?
    A) No Change.
    B) "life. Some"
    C) "life even though some"
    D) "life, still some"

38. Which of the following is the best replacement for the underlined word in sentence 16?
    A) No Change.
    B) "because"
    C) "while"
    D) "since"

39. Which of the following is the best change to the underlined portion in sentence 17?
    A) No Change.
    B) "may only take"
    C) "takes only"
    D) "will only take"

40. Which of the following is the best change to the underlined portion in sentence 18?
    A) No Change.
    B) "citizens will always value"
    C) "will always, be valued by citizens"
    D) "will always be valued by citizens"

Answer Key

1.	A)	21.	A)
2.	C)	22.	B)
3.	D)	23.	B)
4.	D)	24.	A)
5.	D)	25.	B)
6.	D)	26.	B)
7.	B)	27.	B)
8.	D)	28.	B)
9.	D)	29.	C)
10.	C)	30.	C)
11.	B)	31.	B)
12.	A)	32.	A)
13.	C)	33.	C)
14.	A)	34.	D)
15.	C)	35.	D)
16.	D)	36.	D)
17.	C)	37.	C)
18.	B)	38.	A)
19.	A)	39.	B)
20.	D)	40.	D)

MATHEMATICS

THE MOST COMMON MISTAKES

People make little mistakes all the time, but during a test those tiny mistakes can make the difference between a good score and a poor one. Watch out for these common mistakes that people make on the math section of the TABE:

- answering with the wrong sign (positive/negative)
- mixing up the order of operations
- misplacing a decimal
- providing an answer that was not asked for
- circling the wrong letter or filling in wrong circle choice

If you're thinking, *those ideas are just common sense*, that's exactly the point. Most of the mistakes made on the TABE are simple ones. But no matter how silly the mistake, a wrong answer still means a lost point on the test.

STRATEGIES FOR THE MATHEMATICS SECTION

Go Back to the Basics

First and foremost, practice your basic skills: sign changes, order of operations, simplifying fractions, and equation manipulation. These are the skills used most on the TABE, though they are applied in many different contexts. Remember that when it comes down to it, all math problems rely on the four basic skills of addition, subtraction, multiplication, and division. All you need to figure out is the order in which they're used to solve a problem.

Don't Rely on Mental Math

Using mental math is great for eliminating answer choices, but ALWAYS WRITE DOWN YOUR WORK! This cannot be stressed enough. Use whatever paper is provided; by writing and/or drawing out the problem, you are more likely to catch any mistakes. The act of writing things down also forces you to organize your calculations, leading to an improvement in your TABE score.

The Three-Times Rule

You should read each question at least three times to ensure you're using the correct information and answering the right question:

Step one: Read the question and write out the given information.

Step two: Read the question, set up your equation(s), and solve.

Step three: Read the question and check that your answer makes sense (is the amount too large or small; is the answer in the correct unit of measure, etc.).

Make an Educated Guess

Eliminate those answer choices that you are relatively sure are incorrect, and then guess from the remaining choices. Educated guessing is critical to increasing your score.

POSITIVE AND NEGATIVE NUMBERS

You can use a number line to easily find the result when adding and subtracting positive and negative numbers. When adding two numbers, whether they are positive or negative, count to the right; when subtracting, count to the left. Note that adding a negative value is the same as subtracting. Subtracting a negative value is the same as adding.

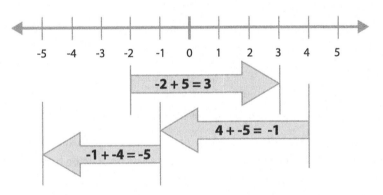

Figure 3.1. Adding and Subtracting Positive and Negative Numbers

Multiplying and dividing with negative and positive numbers is somewhat easier. Multiplying two numbers with the same sign gives a positive result, and multiplying two numbers with different signs gives a negative result. The same rules apply to division. These rules are summarized below:

(+) + (−) = the sign of the larger number

(−) + (−) = negative number

(−) × (−) or (−) ÷ (−) = positive number

(−) × (+) or (−) ÷ (+) = negative number

(+) + (+) or (+) × (+) or (+) ÷ (+) = positive number

Examples

1. Find the product of −10 and 47.

$(-) \times (+) = (-)$

$-10 \times 47 = \textbf{−470}$

2. What is the sum of −65 and −32?

$(-) + (-) = (-)$

$-65 + -32 = \textbf{−97}$

3. Is the product of −7 and 4 less than −7, between −7 and 4, or greater than 4?

$(-) \times (+) = (-)$

$-7 \times 4 = -28$, which is **less than −7**

4. What is the value of −16 divided by 2.5?

$(-) \div (+) = (-)$

$-16 \div 2.5 = \textbf{−6.4}$

ORDER OF OPERATIONS

Operations in a mathematical expression are always performed in a specific order, which is described by the acronym PEMDAS:

1. Parentheses

2. Exponents

3. Multiplication

4. Division

5. Addition

6. Subtraction

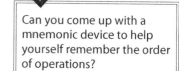

Can you come up with a mnemonic device to help yourself remember the order of operations?

Perform the operations within parentheses first, and then address any exponents. After those steps, perform all multiplication and division. These are carried out from left to right as they appear in the problem.

Finally, do all required addition and subtraction, also from left to right as each operation appears in the problem.

Examples

1. Solve: $-(2)^2 - (4 + 7)$

First, complete operations within parentheses:

$-(2)^2 - (11)$

Second, calculate the value of exponential expressions:

$-(4) - (11)$

Finally, do addition and subtraction:

$-4 - 11 = \textbf{−15}$

2. Solve: $(5)^2 \div 5 + 4 \times 2$

First, calculate the value of exponential expressions:

$(25) \div 5 + 4 \times 2$

Second, calculate division and multiplication from left to right:

$5 + 8$

Finally, do addition and subtraction:

$5 + 8 = \mathbf{13}$

3. Solve the expression: $15 \times (4 + 8) - 3^3$

First, complete operations within parentheses:

$15 \times (12) - 3^3$

Second, calculate the value of exponential expressions:

$15 \times (12) - 27$

Third, calculate division and multiplication from left to right:

$180 - 27$

Finally, do addition and subtraction from left to right:

$180 - 27 = \mathbf{153}$

4. Solve the expression: $\left(\frac{5}{2} \times 4\right) + 23 - 4^2$

First, complete operations within parentheses:

$(10) + 23 - 4^2$

Second, calculate the value of exponential expressions:

$(10) + 23 - 16$

Finally, do addition and subtraction from left to right:

$10 + 23 - 16$

$33 - 16 = \mathbf{17}$

GREATEST COMMON FACTOR

The **GREATEST COMMON FACTOR (GCF)** of a set of numbers is the largest number that can evenly divide into all of the numbers in the set. To find the GCF of a set, find all of the factors of each number in the set. A factor is a whole number that can be multiplied by another whole number to result in the original number. For example, the number 10 has four factors: 1, 2, 5, and 10. (When listing the factors of a number, remember to include 1 and the number itself.) The largest number that is a factor for each number in the set is the GCF.

Examples

1. Find the greatest common factor of 24 and 18.

Factors of 24: 1, 2, 3, 4, 6, 8, 12, 24

Factors of 18: 1, 2, 3, 6, 9, 18

The greatest common factor is 6.

2. Find the greatest common factor of 121 and 44.

Since these numbers are larger, it's easier to start with the smaller number when listing factors.

Factors of 44: 1, 2, 4, 11, 22, 44

Now, it's not necessary to list all of the factors of 121. Instead, we can eliminate those factors of 44 which do not divide evenly into 121:

121 is not evenly divisible by 2, 4, 22, or 44 because it is an odd number. This leaves only 1 and 11 as common factors, so the **GCF is 11**.

3. First aid kits are being assembled at a summer camp. A complete first aid kit requires bandages, sutures, and sterilizing swabs, and each of the kits must be identical to other kits. If the camp's total supplies include 52 bandages, 13 sutures, and 39 sterilizing swabs, how many complete first aid kits can be assembled without having any leftover materials?

This problem is asking for the greatest common factor of 52, 13, and 39. The first step is to find all of the factors of the smallest number, 13.

Factors of 13: 1, 13

13 is a prime number, meaning that its only factors are 1 and itself. Next, we check to see if 13 is also a factor of 39 and 52:

$13 \times 2 = 26$

$13 \times 3 = 39$

$13 \times 4 = 52$

We can see that 39 and 52 are both multiples of 13. This means that **13 first aid kits can be made without having any leftover materials.**

4. Elena is making sundaes for her friends. She has 20 scoops of chocolate ice cream and 16 scoops of strawberry. If she wants to make identical sundaes and use all of her ice cream, how many sundaes can she make?

Arranging things into identical groups with no leftovers is always a tip that the problem calls for finding the greatest common factor. To find the GCF of 16 and 20, the first step is to factor both numbers:

Factors of 16: 1, 2, 4, 8, 16

Factors of 20: 1, 2, 4, 5, 10, 20

From these lists, we see that **4 is the GCF**. Elena can make 4 sundaes, each with 5 scoops of chocolate ice cream and 4 scoops of strawberry. Any other combination would result in leftover ice cream or sundaes that are not identical.

COMPARISON OF RATIONAL NUMBERS

Number comparison problems present numbers in different formats and ask which is larger or smaller, or whether the numbers are equivalent. The important step in solving these problems is to convert the numbers to the same format so that it is easier to see how they compare. If numbers are given in the same format, or after they have been converted, determine which number is smaller or if the numbers are equal. Remember that for negative numbers, higher numbers are actually smaller.

> ⚠ To order numbers from least to greatest (or greatest to least), convert them to the same format and place them on a number line.

Examples

1. Which of the following values is the largest? 0.49, $\frac{3}{5}$, $\frac{1}{2}$, 0.55

   Convert the fractions to decimals:

   $\frac{3}{5} = 0.6$

   $\frac{1}{2} = 0.5$

   Place the values in order from smallest to largest:

   $0.49 < 0.5 < 0.55 < 0.6$

   $\frac{3}{5}$ is the largest number.

2. Place the following numbers in order from least to greatest:

   $\frac{2}{5}$, −0.7, 0.35, −$\frac{3}{2}$, 0.46

   Convert the fractions to decimals:

   $\frac{2}{5} = 0.4$

   $-\frac{3}{2} = -1.5$

   Place the values in order from smallest to largest:

   $-1.5 < -0.7 < 0.35 < 0.4 < 0.46$

   Put the numbers back in their original form:

   $-\frac{3}{2} < -0.7 < 0.35 < \frac{2}{5} < 0.46$

UNITS OF MEASUREMENT

You are expected to memorize some units of measurement. These are given below. When doing unit conversion problems (i.e., when converting one unit to another), find the conversion factor, then apply that factor to the given measurement to find the new units.

Table 3.1. Unit Prefixes

PREFIX	SYMBOL	MULTIPLICATION FACTOR
tera	T	1,000,000,000,000
giga	G	1,000,000,000
mega	M	1,000,000
kilo	k	1,000
hecto	h	100
deca	da	10
base unit	--	--
deci	d	0.1
centi	c	0.01
milli	m	0.001
micro	μ	0.0000001
nano	n	0.0000000001
pico	p	0.0000000000001

Table 3.2. Units and Conversion Factors

DIMENSION	AMERICAN	SI
length	inch/foot/yard/mile	meter
mass	ounce/pound/ton	gram
volume	cup/pint/quart/gallon	liter
force	pound-force	newton
pressure	pound-force per square inch	pascal
work and energy	cal/British thermal unit	joule
temperature	Fahrenheit	kelvin
charge	faraday	coulomb

CONVERSION FACTORS

1 in. = 2.54 cm	1 lb. = 0.454 kg
1 yd. = 0.914 m	1 cal = 4.19 J
1 mi. = 1.61 km	$1°F = \frac{5}{9}(°F - 32°C)$
1 gal. = 3.785 L	$1 cm^3 = 1 mL$
1 oz. = 28.35 g	1 hr = 3600 s

Examples

1. A fence measures 15 ft. long. How many yards long is the fence?

   1 yd. = 3 ft.

   $\frac{15}{3}$ = **5 yd.**

2. A pitcher can hold 24 cups. How many gallons can it hold?

   1 gal. = 16 cups

   $\frac{24}{16}$ = **1.5 gallons**

3. A spool of wire holds 144 in. of wire. If Mario has 3 spools, how many feet of wire does he have?

   12 in. = 1 ft.

   $\frac{144}{12}$ = 12 ft.

   12 ft. × 3 spools = **36 ft. of wire**

4. A ball rolling across a table travels 6 inches per second. How many feet will it travel in 1 minute?

   This problem can be worked in two steps: finding how many inches are covered in 1 minute, and then converting that value to feet. It can also be worked the opposite way, by finding how many feet it travels in 1 second and then converting that to feet traveled per minute. The first method is shown below.

   1 min. = 60 sec.

   (6 in./sec.) × 60 s = 360 in.

   1 ft. = 12 in.

   (360 in./12 in.) = **30 ft.**

5. How many millimeters are in 0.5 m?

1 meter = 1000 mm

0.5 meters = **500 mm**

6. A lead ball weighs 38 g. How many kilograms does it weigh?

1 kg = 1000 g

$\frac{38}{1000}$ g = **0.038 kg**

7. How many cubic centimeters are in 10 L?

1 L = 1000 ml

10 L = 1000 ml × 10

10 L = **10,000 ml or cm³**

8. Jennifer's pencil was initially 10 centimeters long. After she sharpened it, it was 9.6 centimeters long. How many millimeters did she lose from her pencil by sharpening it?

1 cm = 10 mm

10 cm – 9.6 cm = 0.4 cm lost

0.4 cm = 10 × .4 mm = **4 mm were lost**

DECIMALS AND FRACTIONS

Numbers are written using the base-10 system where each digit (the numeric symbols 0 – 9) in a number is worth ten times as much as the number to the right of it. For example, in the number 37 each digit has a place value based on its location. The 3 is in the tens place, and so has a value of 30, and the 7 is in the ones place, so it has a value of 7.

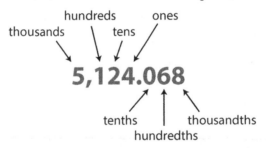

Figure 3.2. Place Value

Adding and Subtracting Decimals

When adding and subtracting decimals, write the numbers so that the decimal points are aligned. You want to subtract the ones place from the ones place, the tenths place from the tenths place, etc.

Examples

1. Find the sum of 17.07 and 2.52.

```
   17.07
+   2.52
= 19.59
```

2. Jeannette has 7.4 gallons of gas in her tank. After driving, she has 6.8 gallons. How many gallons of gas did she use?

7.4

− 6.8

= **0.6 gal.**

Multiplying and Dividing Decimals

When multiplying decimals, start by multiplying the numbers normally. You can then determine the placement of the decimal point in the result by adding the number of digits after the decimal in each of the numbers you multiplied together.

When dividing decimals, you should move the decimal point in the divisor (the number you're dividing by) until it is a whole number. You can then move the decimal in the dividend (the number you're dividing into) the same number of places in the same direction. Finally, divide the new numbers normally to get the correct answer.

Examples

1. What is the product of 0.25 and 1.3?

$25 \times 13 = 325$

There are 2 digits after the decimal in 0.25 and one digit after the decimal in 1.3. Therefore the product should have 3 digits after the decimal: 0.325.

2. Find $0.8 \div 0.2$.

Change 0.2 to 2 by moving the decimal one space to the right.

Next, move the decimal one space to the right on the dividend. 0.8 becomes 8.

Now, divide 8 by 2. $8 \div 2 = \mathbf{4}$

3. Find the quotient when 40 is divided by 0.25.

First, change the divisor to a whole number: 0.25 becomes 25.

Next, change the dividend to match the divisor by moving the decimal two spaces to the right, so 40 becomes 4000.

Now divide: $4000 \div 25 = \mathbf{160}$

Working with Fractions

FRACTIONS are made up of two parts: the NUMERATOR, which appears above the bar, and the DENOMINATOR, which is below it. If a fraction is in its SIMPLEST FORM, the numerator and the denominator share no common factors. A fraction with a numerator larger than or equal to its denominator is an IMPROPER FRACTION; when the denominator is larger, it's a PROPER FRACTION.

Improper fractions can be converted into mixed numbers by dividing the numerator by the denominator. The resulting whole number is placed to the left of the fraction, and the remainder becomes the new numerator; the denominator does not change. The new number is called a MIXED NUMBER because it contains a whole number and a fraction. Mixed numbers can be turned into improper fractions through the reverse process: multiply the whole number by the denominator and add the numerator to get the new numerator.

Examples

1. Simplify the fraction $\frac{121}{77}$.

121 and 77 share a common factor of 11. So, if we divide each by 11 we can simplify the fraction:

$$\frac{121}{77} = \frac{11}{11} \times \frac{11}{7} = \mathbf{\frac{11}{7}}$$

2. Convert $\frac{37}{5}$ into a mixed number.

Start by dividing the numerator by the denominator:

$37 \div 5 = 7$ with a remainder of 2

Now build a mixed number with the whole number and the new numerator:

$$\frac{37}{5} = \mathbf{7\frac{2}{5}}$$

Multiplying and Dividing Fractions

To multiply fractions, convert any mixed numbers into improper fractions and multiply the numerators together and the denominators together. Reduce to lowest terms if needed.

> Inverting a fraction changes division to multiplication:
> $$\frac{a}{b} \div \frac{c}{d} = \frac{a}{b} \times \frac{d}{c} = \frac{ad}{bc}$$

To divide fractions, first convert any mixed numbers into improper fractions. Then, invert the second fraction so that the denominator and numerator are switched. Finally, multiply the numerators together and the denominators together.

Examples

1. What is the product of $\frac{1}{12}$ and $\frac{6}{8}$?

Simply multiply the numerators together and the denominators together, then reduce:

$$\frac{1}{12} \times \frac{6}{8} = \frac{6}{96} = \mathbf{\frac{1}{16}}$$

Sometimes it's easier to reduce fractions before multiplying if you can:

$$\frac{1}{12} \times \frac{6}{8} = \frac{1}{12} \times \frac{3}{4} = \frac{3}{48} = \mathbf{\frac{1}{16}}$$

2. Find $\frac{7}{8} \div \frac{1}{4}$.

For a fraction division problem, invert the second fraction and then multiply and reduce:

$$\frac{7}{8} \div \frac{1}{4} = \frac{7}{8} \times \frac{4}{1} = \frac{28}{8} = \mathbf{\frac{7}{2}}$$

3. $\frac{2}{5} \div 1\frac{1}{5} =$

This is a fraction division problem, so the first step is to convert the mixed number to an improper fraction:

$$1\frac{1}{5} = \frac{5 \times 1}{5} + \frac{1}{5} = \frac{6}{5}$$

Now, divide the fractions. Remember to invert the second fraction, and then multiply normally:

$$\frac{2}{5} \div \frac{6}{5} = \frac{2}{5} \times \frac{5}{6} = \frac{10}{30} = \mathbf{\frac{1}{3}}$$

4. A recipe calls for $\frac{1}{4}$ cup of sugar. If $8\frac{1}{2}$ batches of the recipe are needed, how many cups of sugar will be used?

This is a fraction multiplication problem: $\frac{1}{4} \times 8\frac{1}{2}$.

First, we need to convert the mixed number into a proper fraction:

$$8\frac{1}{2} = \frac{8 \times 2}{2} + \frac{1}{2} = \frac{17}{2}$$

Now, multiply the fractions across the numerators and denominators, and then reduce:

$$\frac{1}{4} \times 8\frac{1}{2} = \frac{1}{4} \times \frac{17}{2} = \mathbf{\frac{17}{8}} \text{ cups of sugar, or } \mathbf{2\frac{1}{8}}$$

Adding and Subtracting Fractions

Adding and subtracting fractions requires a **COMMON DENOMINATOR**. To get a common denominator, you can multiply each fraction by the number 1. With fractions, any number over itself (e.g., $\frac{5}{5}$, $\frac{12}{12}$, etc.) is equivalent to 1, so multiplying by such a fraction can change the denominator without changing the value of the fraction. Once the denominators are the same, the numerators can be added or subtracted.

To add mixed numbers, you can first add the whole numbers and then the fractions. To subtract mixed numbers, convert each mixed number to an improper fraction, get a common denominator, and then subtract the numerators.

Examples

1. Simplify the expression $\frac{2}{3} - \frac{1}{5}$.

First, multiply each fraction by a factor of 1 to get a common denominator. How do you know which factor of 1 to use? Look at the other fraction and use the number found in that denominator:

$$\frac{2}{3} - \frac{1}{5} = \frac{2}{3}\left(\frac{5}{5}\right) - \frac{1}{5}\left(\frac{3}{3}\right) = \frac{10}{15} - \frac{3}{15}$$

Once the fractions have a common denominator, simply subtract the numerators:

$$\frac{10}{15} - \frac{3}{15} = \mathbf{\frac{7}{15}}$$

The phrase *simplify the expression* just means you need to perform all the operations in the expression.

2. Find $2\frac{1}{3} - \frac{3}{2}$.

This is a fraction subtraction problem with a mixed number, so the first step is to convert the mixed number to an improper fraction:

$$2\frac{1}{3} = \frac{2 \times 3}{3} + \frac{1}{3} = \frac{7}{3}$$

Next, convert each fraction so they share a common denominator:

$$\frac{7}{3} \times \frac{2}{2} = \frac{14}{6}$$
$$\frac{3}{2} \times \frac{3}{3} = \frac{9}{6}$$

Now, subtract the fractions by subtracting the numerators:

$$\frac{14}{6} - \frac{9}{6} = \mathbf{\frac{5}{6}}$$

3. Find the sum of $\frac{9}{16}$, $\frac{1}{2}$, and $\frac{7}{4}$.

For this fraction addition problem, we need to find a common denominator. Notice that 2 and 4 are both factors of 16, so 16 can be the common denominator:

$$\frac{1}{2} \times \frac{8}{8} = \frac{8}{16}$$

$$\frac{7}{4} \times \frac{4}{4} = \frac{28}{16}$$

$$\frac{9}{16} + \frac{8}{16} + \frac{28}{16} = \mathbf{\frac{45}{16}}$$

4. Sabrina has $\frac{2}{3}$ of a can of red paint. Her friend Amos has $\frac{1}{6}$ of a can. How much red paint do they have combined?

To add fractions, make sure that they have a common denominator. Since 3 is a factor of 6, 6 can be the common denominator:

$$\frac{2}{3} \times \frac{2}{2} = \frac{4}{6}$$

Now, add the numerators:

$$\frac{4}{6} + \frac{1}{6} = \mathbf{\frac{5}{6}} \textbf{ of a can}$$

Converting Decimals to Fractions

To convert a decimal, simply use the numbers that come after the decimal as the numerator in the fraction. The denominator will be a power of 10 that matches the place value for the original decimal. For example, the denominator for 0.46 would be 100 because the last number is in the hundredths place; likewise, the denominator for 0.657 would be 1000 because the last number is in the thousandths place. Once this fraction has been set up, all that's left is to simplify it.

To convert a fraction to a decimal, just divide the numerator by the denominator on your calculator.

Example

Convert 0.45 into a fraction.

The last number in the decimal is in the hundredths place, so we can easily set up a fraction:

$$0.45 = \frac{45}{100}$$

The next step is to simply reduce the fraction down to the lowest common denominator. Here, both 45 and 100 are divisible by 5:

$$\frac{45}{100} = \frac{(45 \div 5)}{(100 \div 5)} = \mathbf{\frac{9}{20}}$$

RATIOS

A RATIO tells you how many of one thing exist in relation to the number of another thing. Unlike fractions, ratios do not give a part relative to a whole; instead, they compare two values. For example, if you have 3 apples and 4 oranges, the ratio of apples to oranges is 3 to 4. Ratios can be written using words (3 to 4), fractions $\left(\frac{3}{4}\right)$, or colons (3:4).

In order to work with ratios, it's helpful to rewrite them as a fraction expressing a part to a whole. For example, in the example above you have 7 total pieces of fruit, so the fraction of your fruit that are apples is $\frac{3}{7}$, and oranges make up $\frac{4}{7}$ of your fruit collection.

One last important thing to consider when working with ratios is the units of the values being compared. On the TABE, you may be asked to rewrite a ratio using the same units on both sides. For example, you might have to rewrite the ratio 3 minutes to 7 seconds as 180 seconds to 7 seconds.

Examples

1. There are 90 voters in a room, and each is either a Democrat or a Republican. The ratio of Democrats to Republicans is 5:4. How many Republicans are there?

    We know that there are 5 Democrats for every 4 Republicans in the room, which means for every 9 people, 4 are Republicans.

    $5 + 4 = 9$

    Fraction of Republicans: $\frac{4}{9}$

    If $\frac{4}{9}$ of the 90 voters are Republicans, then:

    $\frac{4}{9} \times 90 = $ **40 voters are Republicans**

2. The ratio of students to teachers in a school is 15:1. If there are 38 teachers, how many students attend the school?

    To solve this ratio problem, we can simply multiply both sides of the ratio by the desired value to find the number of students that correspond to having 38 teachers:

    $\frac{15 \text{ students}}{1 \text{ teacher}} \times 38 \text{ teachers} = 570 \text{ students}$

    The school has **570 students**.

PROPORTIONS

A **PROPORTION** is an equation which states that 2 ratios are equal. Proportions are usually written as 2 fractions joined by an equal sign $\left(\frac{a}{b} = \frac{c}{d}\right)$, but they can also be written using colons ($a : b :: c : d$). Note that in a proportion, the units must be the same in both numerators and in both denominators.

Often you will be given 3 of the values in a proportion and asked to find the 4th. In these types of problems, you can solve for the missing variable by cross-multiplying—multiply the numerator of each fraction by the denominator of the other to get an equation with no fractions as shown below. You can then solve the equation using basic algebra. (For more on solving basic equations, see "Algebraic Expressions and Equations.")

Proportion problems on the TABE are usually word problems that include: distance and time, cost, or measurement.

$$\frac{a}{b} = \frac{c}{d} \rightarrow ad = bc$$

Examples

1. A train traveling 120 miles takes 3 hours to get to its destination. How long will it take for the train to travel 180 miles?

    Start by setting up the proportion:

    $\frac{120 \text{ miles}}{3 \text{ hours}} = \frac{180 \text{ miles}}{x \text{ hours}}$

Note that it doesn't matter which value is placed in the numerator or denominator, as long as it is the same on both sides. Now, solve for the missing quantity through cross–multiplication:

120 miles × x hours = 3 hours × 180 miles

Now solve the equation:

$$x \text{ hours} = \frac{(3 \text{ hours}) \times (180 \text{ miles})}{120 \text{ miles}}$$

x = 4.5 hours

2. One acre of wheat requires 500 gallons of water. How many acres can be watered with 2600 gallons?

Set up the equation:

$$\frac{1 \text{ acre}}{500 \text{ gal.}} = \frac{x \text{ acres}}{2600 \text{ gal.}}$$

Then solve for x:

$$x \text{ acres} = \frac{1 \text{ acre} \times 2600 \text{ gal.}}{500 \text{ gal.}}$$

$$x = \frac{26}{5} \text{ or } \textbf{5.2 acres}$$

PERCENTAGES

A **PERCENT** is the ratio of a part to the whole multiplied by 100. The equation for percentages can be rearranged to solve for either the part, the whole, or the percent:

$$percent = \frac{part}{whole}$$
$$part = whole \times percent$$
$$whole = \frac{part}{percent}$$

In the equations above, the percent should always be expressed as a decimal. In order to convert a decimal into a percentage value, simply multiply it by 100. So, if you've read 5 pages (the part) of a 10-page article (the whole), you've read $\frac{5}{10}$ = 0.5 = 50%. (The percent sign (%) is used once the decimal has been multiplied by 100.)

Note that when solving these problems, the units for the part and the whole should be the same. If you're reading a book, saying you've read 5 pages out of 15 chapters doesn't make any sense.

⚠ The word *of* usually indicates what the whole is in a problem. For example, the problem might say *Ella ate two slices of the pizza*, which means the pizza is the whole.

Examples

1. 45 is 15% of what number?

   Set up the appropriate equation and solve. Don't forget to change 15% to a decimal value:

   $$whole = \frac{part}{percent} = \frac{45}{0.15} = \textbf{300}$$

2. Jim spent 30% of his paycheck at the fair. He spent $15 for a hat, $30 for a shirt, and $20 playing games. How much was his check? (Round to nearest dollar.)

   Set up the appropriate equation and solve:

   $$whole = \frac{part}{percent} = \frac{15 + 30 + 20}{.30} = \textbf{\$217.00}$$

3. What percent of 65 is 39?

Set up the equation and solve:

$percent = \frac{part}{whole} = \frac{39}{65} = $ **0.6 or 60%**

4. Greta and Max sell cable subscriptions. In a given month, Greta sells 45 subscriptions and Max sells 51. If 240 total subscriptions were sold in that month, what percent were not sold by Greta or Max?

You can use the information in the question to figure out what percentage of subscriptions were sold by Max and Greta:

$percent = \frac{part}{whole} = \frac{(51 + 45)}{240} = \frac{96}{240} = 0.4$ or 40%

However, the question asks how many subscriptions weren't sold by Max or Greta. If they sold 40%, then the other salespeople sold 100% − 40% = **60%**.

5. Grant needs to score 75% on an exam. If the exam has 45 questions, how many questions does he need to answer correctly?

Set up the equation and solve. Remember to convert 75% to a decimal value:

$part = whole \times percent = 45 \times 0.75 = 33.75$, so he needs to answer at least **34 questions correctly**.

PERCENT CHANGE

PERCENT CHANGE problems will ask you to calculate how much a given quantity changed. The problems are solved in a similar way to regular percent problems, except that instead of using the *part* you'll use the *amount of change*. Note that the sign of the *amount of change* is important: if the original amount has increased the change will be positive, and if it has decreased the change will be negative. Again, in the equations below the percent is a decimal value; you need to multiply by 100 to get the actual percentage.

Words that indicate a percent change problem: *discount, markup, sale, increase, decrease*

$$percent\ change = \frac{amount\ of\ change}{original\ amount}$$
$$amount\ of\ change = original\ amount \times percent\ change$$
$$original\ amount = \frac{amount\ of\ change}{percent\ change}$$

Examples

1. A computer software retailer marks up its games by 40% above the wholesale price when it sells them to customers. Find the price of a game for a customer if the game costs the retailer $25.

Set up the appropriate equation and solve:

amount of change = original amount × percent change = 25 × 0.4 = 10

If the amount of change is 10, that means the store adds a markup of $10, so the game costs:

$25 + $10 = **$35**

2. A golf shop pays its wholesaler $40 for a certain club, and then sells it to a golfer for $75. What is the markup rate?

First, calculate the amount of change:

$75 - 40 = 35$

Now you can set up the equation and solve. (Note that *markup rate* is another way of saying *percent change*):

$percent\ change = \dfrac{amount\ of\ change}{original\ amount} = \dfrac{35}{40} = 0.875 = \textbf{87.5\%}$

3. A store charges a 40% markup on the shoes it sells. How much did the store pay for a pair of shoes purchased by a customer for $63?

You're solving for the original price, but it's going to be tricky because you don't know the amount of change; you only know the new price. To solve, you need to create an expression for the amount of change:

If *original amount* $= x$

Then *amount of change* $= 63 - x$

Now you can plug these values into your equation:

$original\ amount = \dfrac{amount\ of\ change}{percent\ change}$

$x = \dfrac{63 - x}{0.4}$

The last step is to solve for x:

$0.4x = 63 - x$

$1.4x = 63$

$x = 45$

The store paid **$45 for the shoes**.

4. An item originally priced at $55 is marked 25% off. What is the sale price?

You've been asked to find the sale price, which means you need to solve for the amount of change first:

amount of change = original amount × percent change =

$55 \times 0.25 = 13.75$

Using this amount, you can find the new price. Because it's on sale, we know the item will cost less than the original price:

$55 - 13.75 = 41.25$

The sale price is $41.25.

PROBABILITIES

A PROBABILITY is found by dividing the number of desired outcomes by the number of total possible outcomes. As with percentages, a probability is the ratio of a part to a whole, with the whole being the total number of things that could happen, and the part being the number of those things that would be considered a success. Probabilities can be written using percentages (40%), decimals (0.4), fractions $\left(\frac{2}{5}\right)$, or in words (probability is 2 in 5).

$$probability = \dfrac{desired\ outcomes}{total\ possible\ outcomes}$$

Examples

1. A bag holds 3 blue marbles, 5 green marbles, and 7 red marbles. If you pick one marble from the bag, what is the probability it will be blue?

   Because there are 15 marbles in the bag (3 + 5 + 7), the total number of possible outcomes is 15. Of those outcomes, 3 would be blue marbles, which is the desired outcome. With that information you can set up an equation:

   $$\text{probability} = \frac{\text{desired outcomes}}{\text{total possible outcomes}} = \frac{3}{15} = \frac{1}{5}$$

   The probability is 1 in 5 or 0.2 that a blue marble is picked.

2. A bag contains 75 balls. If the probability that a ball selected from the bag will be red is 0.6, how many red balls are in the bag?

   Because you're solving for desired outcomes (the number of red balls), first you need to rearrange the equation:

   $$\text{probability} = \frac{\text{desired outcomes}}{\text{total possible outcomes}}$$

   desired outcomes = probability × total possible outcomes

   In this problem, the desired outcome is choosing a red ball, and the total possible outcomes are represented by the 75 total balls.

   desired outcomes = 0.6 × 75 = 45

   There are 45 red balls in the bag.

3. A theater has 230 seats: 75 seats are in the orchestra area, 100 seats are in the mezzanine, and 55 seats are in the balcony. If a ticket is selected at random, what is the probability that it will be for either a mezzanine or balcony seat?

   In this problem, the desired outcome is a seat in either the mezzanine or balcony area, and the total possible outcomes are represented by the 230 total seats, so the equation should be written as:

   $$\text{probability} = \frac{\text{desired outcomes}}{\text{total possible outcomes}} = \frac{100 + 55}{230} = \textbf{0.67}$$

4. The probability of selecting a student whose name begins with the letter s from a school attendance log is 7%. If there are 42 students whose names begin with s enrolled at the school, how many students attend the school?

   Because you're solving for total possible outcomes (total number of students), first you need to rearrange the equation:

   $$\text{probability} = \frac{\text{desired outcomes}}{\text{total possible outcomes}}$$

   $$\text{total possible outcomes} = \frac{\text{desired outcomes}}{\text{probability}}$$

   In this problem, you are given a probability (7% or 0.07) and the number of desired outcomes (42). These can be plugged into the equation to solve:

   $$\text{total possible outcomes} = \frac{\text{desired outcomes}}{\text{probability}} = \frac{42}{0.07} = \textbf{600 students}$$

ALGEBRAIC EXPRESSIONS AND EQUATIONS

Algebraic expressions and equations include a VARIABLE, which is a letter standing in for a number. These expressions and equations are made up of TERMS, which are groups of numbers and variables (e.g., $2xy$). An EXPRESSION is simply a set of terms (e.g., $3x + 2xy$), while an EQUATION includes an equal sign (e.g., $3x + 2xy = 17$). When simplifying expressions or solving algebraic equations, you'll need to use many different mathematical properties and operations, including addition, subtraction, multiplication, division, exponents, roots, distribution, and the order of operations.

Evaluating Algebraic Expressions

To evaluate an algebraic expression, simply plug the given value(s) in for the appropriate variable(s) in the expression.

Examples

1. Evaluate $2x + 6y - 3z$ if $x = 2$, $y = 4$, and $z = -3$.

   Plug in each number for the correct variable and simplify:

   $2x + 6y - 3z = 2(2) + 6(4) - 3(-3) = 4 + 24 + 9 = \mathbf{37}$

2. A hat company's profits are described by the expression below, where x is the number of hats sold, and p is the average price of a hat.

   $xp - 5x - 5000$

   If the company sold 10,000 hats for $13 each, what was its profit?

   Identify the variables:

   $x = 10,000$

   $p = \$13$

   Plug these values into the given expression:

   $xp - 5x - 5000$

   $= (10,000)(13) - 5(10,000) - 5000 = \mathbf{\$75,000}$

Adding and Subtracting Terms

Only LIKE TERMS, which have the exact same variable(s), can be added or subtracted. CONSTANTS are numbers without variables attached, and those can be added and subtracted together as well. When simplifying an expression, like terms should be added or subtracted so that no individual group of variables occurs in more than one term. For example, the expression $5x + 6xy$ is in its simplest form, while $5x + 6xy - 11xy$ is not because xy appears in more than one term.

Example

1. Simplify the expression $5xy + 7y + 2yz + 11xy - 5yz$.

   Start by grouping together like terms:

   $(5xy + 11xy) + (2yz - 5yz) + 7y$

   Now you can add together each set of like terms:

   $\mathbf{16xy - 3yz + 7y}$

2. Simplify the expression: $3ac + 4ab^2 - bc + 2ac - 7bc + 3a^3bc$

   Start by grouping like terms together, then add together each set of like terms:

   $(3ac + 2ac) + (-bc - 7bc) + 4ab^2 + 3a^3bc$

   $= \mathbf{5ac - 8bc + 4ab^2 + 3a^3bc}$

Multiplying and Dividing Terms

To multiply a single term by another, simply multiply the coefficients and then multiply the variables. Remember that when multiplying variables with exponents, those exponents are added together. For example, $(x^5 y)(x^3 y^4) = x^8 y^5$.

When multiplying a term by a set of terms inside parentheses, you need to **DISTRIBUTE** to each term inside the parentheses as shown in Figure 3.3.

$$\mathbf{a(b+c) = ab + ac}$$

Figure 3.3. Distribution

When variables occur in both the numerator and denominator of a fraction, they cancel each other out. So, a fraction with variables in its simplest form will not have the same variable on the top and bottom.

Examples

1. Simplify the expression $(3x^4 y^2 z)(2y^4 z^5)$.

   Multiply the coefficients and variables together:

   $3 \times 2 = 6$

   $y^2 \times y^4 = y^6$

   $z \times z^5 = z^6$

   Now put all the terms back together:

   $\mathbf{6x^4 y^6 z^6}$

2. Simplify the expression: $(2y^2)(y^3 + 2xy^2 z + 4z)$

   Multiply each term inside the parentheses by the term $2y^2$:

   $(2y^2)(y^3 + 2xy^2 z + 4z)$

   $(2y^2 \times y^3) + (2y^2 \times 2xy^2 z) + (2y^2 \times 4z)$

   $\mathbf{2y^5 + 4xy^4 z + 8y^2 z}$

3. Simplify the expression: $\dfrac{2x^4 y^3 z}{8x^2 z^2}$

   Simplify by looking at each variable and crossing out those that appear in the numerator and denominator:

   $\dfrac{2}{8} = \dfrac{1}{4}$

   $\dfrac{x^4}{x^2} = \dfrac{x^2}{1}$

   $\dfrac{z}{z^2} = \dfrac{1}{z}$

   $\dfrac{2x^4 y^3 z}{8x^2 z^2} = \dfrac{x^2 y^3}{4z}$

When multiplying terms with the same base, add the exponents. When dividing terms with the same base, subtract the exponents.

Solving Equations

To solve an equation, you need to manipulate the terms on each side to isolate the variable, meaning if you want to find x, you have to get the x alone on one side of the equal sign. To do this, you'll need to use many of the tools discussed above: you might need to distribute, divide, add, or subtract like terms, or find common denominators.

Think of each side of the equation as the two sides of a see-saw. As long as the two people on each end weigh the same amount the see-saw will be balanced: if you have a 120 lb. person on each end, the see-saw is balanced. Giving each of them a 10 lb. rock to hold changes the weight on each end, but the see-saw itself stays balanced. Equations work the same way: you can add, subtract, multiply, or divide whatever you want as long as you do the same thing to both sides.

Most equations you'll see on the TABE can be solved using the same basic steps:

1. Distribute to get rid of parentheses.
2. Use the least common denominator to get rid of fractions.
3. Add/subtract like terms on either side.
4. Add/subtract so that constants appear on only one side of the equation.
5. Multiply/divide to isolate the variable.

Examples

1. Solve for x: $25x + 12 = 62$

   This equation has no parentheses, fractions, or like terms on the same side, so you can start by subtracting 12 from both sides of the equation:

   $25x + 12 = 62$

   $(25x + 12) - 12 = 62 - 12$

   $25x = 50$

   Now, divide by 25 to isolate the variable:

   $\frac{25x}{25} = \frac{50}{25}$

   $x = 2$

2. Solve the following equation for x: $2x - 4(2x + 3) = 24$

   Start by distributing to get rid of the parentheses (don't forget to distribute the negative):

   $2x - 4(2x + 3) = 24$

   $2x - 8x - 12 = 24$

   There are no fractions, so now you can join like terms:

   $2x - 8x - 12 = 24$

   $-6x - 12 = 24$

   Now add 12 to both sides and divide by −6.

   $-6x - 12 = 24$

   $(-6x - 12) + 12 = 24 + 12$

   $-6x = 36$

   $\frac{-6x}{-6} = \frac{36}{-6}$

   $x = -6$

3. Solve the following equation for x: $\frac{x}{3} + \frac{1}{2} = \frac{x}{6} - \frac{5}{12}$

   Start by multiplying by the least common denominator to get rid of the fractions:

   $\frac{x}{3} + \frac{1}{2} = \frac{x}{6} - \frac{5}{12}$

   $12\left(\frac{x}{3} + \frac{1}{2}\right) = 12\left(\frac{x}{6} - \frac{5}{12}\right)$

   $4x + 6 = 2x - 5$

Now you can isolate x:

$(4x + 6) - 6 = (2x - 5) - 6$

$4x = 2x - 11$

$(4x) - 2x = (2x - 11) - 2x$

$2x = -11$

$x = -\dfrac{11}{2}$

4. Solve for x: $2(x + y) - 7x = 14x + 3$

This equation looks more difficult because it has 2 variables, but you can use the same steps to solve for x. First, distribute to get rid of the parentheses and combine like terms:

$2(x + y) - 7x = 14x + 3$

$2x + 2y - 7x = 14x + 3$

$-5x + 2y = 14x + 3$

Now you can move the x terms to one side and everything else to the other, and then divide to isolate x:

$-5x + 2y = 14x + 3$

$-19x = -2y + 3$

$x = \dfrac{2y - 3}{19}$

INEQUALITIES

INEQUALITIES look like equations, except that instead of having an equal sign, they have one of the following symbols:

> Greater than: The expression left of the symbol is larger than the expression on the right.

< Less than: The expression left of the symbol is smaller than the expression on the right.

≥ Greater than or equal to: The expression left of the symbol is larger than or equal to the expression on the right.

≤ Less than or equal to: The expression left of the symbol is less than or equal to the expression on the right.

Inequalities are solved like linear and algebraic equations. The only difference is that the symbol must be reversed when both sides of the equation are multiplied or divided by a negative number.

Example

1. Solve for x: $-7x + 2 < 6 - 5x$

Collect like terms on each side as you would for a regular equation:

$-7x + 2 < 6 - 5x$

$-2x < 4$

The direction of the sign switches when you divide by a negative number:

$-2x < 4$

$x > -2$

2. A man is building a garden with an area, A, given by the equation below, where a, b, and c are the lengths of three sides of the garden:

$A = ab + bc - ac$

If he needs the garden to be less than 50 square feet, can he build a garden with side lengths of $a = 5$ ft, $b = 7$ ft, and $c = 3$ ft?

The question includes the phrase less than, indicating it's an inequality problem. First, set up the inequality:

$ab + bc - ac < A$

Next, plug the given values in to see if the inequality is true:

$50 > 5(7) + 7(3) - 5(3)$

$50 > 41$

The inequality is true, so he can build the garden.

ABSOLUTE VALUE

The **ABSOLUTE VALUE** of a number (represented by the symbol $|x|$) is its distance from zero, not its value. For example, $|3| = 3$, and $|-3| = 3$ because both 3 and -3 are three units from zero. The absolute value of a number is always positive.

Equations with absolute values will have two answers, so you need to set up two equations. The first is simply the equation with the absolute value symbol removed. For the second equation, isolate the absolute value on one side of the equation and multiply the other side of the equation by -1.

Examples

1. Solve for x: $|2x - 3| = x + 1$

   Set up the first equation by removing the absolute value symbol, then solve for x:

   $|2x - 3| = x + 1$

   $2x - 3 = x + 1$

   $x = 4$

   For the second equation, remove the absolute value and multiply by -1:

   $|2x - 3| = x + 1$

   $2x - 3 = -(x + 1)$

   $2x - 3 = -x - 1$

   $3x = 2$

   $x = \frac{2}{3}$

   Both answers are correct, so the complete answer is **$x = 4$ or $\frac{2}{3}$.**

2. Solve for y: $2|y + 4| = 10$

   Set up the first equation:

   $2(y + 4) = 10$

$y + 4 = 5$

$y = 1$

Set up the second equation. Remember to isolate the absolute value before multiplying by −1:

$2|y + 4| = 10$

$|y + 4| = 5$

$y + 4 = -5$

$y = -9$

$y = 1$ or -9

SOLVING WORD PROBLEMS

Any of the math concepts discussed here can be turned into a word problem, and you'll likely see word problems in various forms throughout the test. (In fact, you may have noticed that several examples in the ratio and proportion sections were word problems.)

The most important step in solving any word problem is to read the entire problem before beginning to solve it: one of the most commonly made mistakes on word problems is providing an answer to a question that wasn't asked. Also, remember that not all of the information given in a problem is always needed to solve it.

When working multiple-choice word problems like those on the TABE, it's important to check your answer. Many of the incorrect choices will be answers that test takers arrive at by making common mistakes. So even if an answer you calculated is given as an answer choice, that doesn't necessarily mean you've worked the problem correctly—you have to check your own work to make sure. General steps for word problems are:

- Step 1: Read the entire problem and determine what the question is asking for.
- Step 2: List all of the given data and define the variables.
- Step 3: Determine the formula(s) needed or set up equations from the information in the problem.
- Step 4: Solve.
- Step 5: Check your answer. (Is the amount too large or small? Are the answers in the correct unit of measure?)

Word problems generally contain key words that can help you determine what math processes may be required in order to solve them.

- Addition: added, combined, increased by, in all, total, perimeter, sum, and more than
- Subtraction: how much more, less than, fewer than, exceeds, difference, and decreased
- Multiplication: of, times, area, and product
- Division: distribute, share, average, per, out of, percent, and quotient
- Equals: is, was, are, amounts to, and were

Basic Word Problems

A word problem in algebra is just an equation or a set of equations described using words. Your task when solving these problems is to turn the "story" of the problem into mathematical equations.

Examples

1. A store owner bought a case of 48 backpacks for $476.00. He sold 17 of the backpacks in his store for $18 each, and the rest were sold to a school for $15 each. What was the salesman's profit?

   Start by listing all the data and defining the variable:

   total number of backpacks = 48

   cost of backpacks = $476.00

   backpacks sold in store at price of $18 = 17

   backpacks sold to school at a price of $15 = 48 − 17 = 31

   total profit = x

   Now set up an equation:

   total profit = income − cost = (306 + 465) − 476 = 295

   The store owner made a profit of **$295**.

2. Thirty students in Mr. Joyce's room are working on projects over 2 days. The first day, he gave them $\frac{3}{5}$ hour to work. On the second day, he gave them half as much time as the first day. How much time did each student have to work on the project?

   Start by listing all the data and defining your variables. Note that the number of students, while given in the problem, is not needed to find the answer:

   time on 1st day = $\frac{3}{5}$ hour = 36 min.

   time on 2nd day = $\frac{1}{2}$(36) = 18 min.

   total time = x

   Now set up the equation and solve:

   total time = time on 1st day + time on 2nd day

   x = 36 + 18 = 54

   The students had 54 minutes to work on the projects.

Distance Word Problems

Distance word problems involve something traveling at a constant or average speed. Whenever you read a problem that involves *how fast*, *how far*, or *for how long*, you should think of the distance equation, $d = rt$, where *d* stands for distance, *r* for rate (speed), and *t* for time.

These problems can be solved by setting up a grid with d, r, and t along the top and each moving object on the left. When setting up the grid, make sure the units are consistent. For example, if the distance is in meters and the time is in seconds, the rate should be meters per second.

Examples

1. Will drove from his home to the airport at an average speed of 30 mph. He then boarded a helicopter and flew to the hospital with an average speed of 60 mph. The entire distance was 150 miles, and the trip took 3 hours. Find the distance from the airport to the hospital.

   The first step is to set up a table and fill in a value for each variable:

   DRIVE TIME

	d	r	t
driving	d	30	t
flying	$150 - d$	60	$3 - t$

   You can now set up equations for driving and flying. The first row gives the equation $d = 30t$, and the second row gives the equation $150 - d = 60(3 - t)$.

   Next, you can solve this system of equations. Start by substituting for d in the second equation:

   $d = 30t$

   $150 - d = 60(3 - t) \rightarrow 150 - 30t = 60(3 - t)$

   Now solve for t:

   $150 - 30t = 180 - 60t$

   $-30 = -30t$

   $1 = t$

   Although you've solved for t, you're not done yet. Notice that the problem asks for distance. So, you need to solve for d. It does not ask for time, but the time is needed to solve the problem.

   Driving: $30t = 30$ miles

   Flying: $150 - d = 120$ miles

   The distance from the airport to the hospital is 120 miles.

2. Two cyclists start at the same time from opposite ends of a course that is 45 miles long. One cyclist is riding at 14 mph and the second cyclist is riding at 16 mph. How long after they begin will they meet?

   First, set up the table. The variable for time will be the same for each, because they will have been on the road for the same amount of time when they meet:

   CYCLIST TIMES

	d	r	t
Cyclist #1	d	14	t
Cyclist #2	$45 - d$	16	t

   Next set up two equations:

   Cyclist #1: $d = 14t$

   Cyclist #2: $45 - d = 16t$

   Now substitute and solve:

   $d = 14t$

   $45 - d = 16t \rightarrow 45 - 14t = 16t$

$45 = 30t$

$t = 1.5$

They will meet 1.5 hr. after they begin.

Work Problems

WORK PROBLEMS involve situations where several people or machines are doing work at different rates. Your task is usually to figure out how long it will take these people or machines to complete a task while working together. The trick to doing work problems is to figure out how much of the project each person or machine completes in the same unit of time. For example, you might calculate how much of a wall a person can paint in 1 hour, or how many boxes an assembly line can pack in 1 minute.

Once you know that, you can set up an equation to solve for the total time. This equation usually has a form similar to the equation for distance, but here *work = rate × time*.

Examples

1. Bridget can clean an entire house in 12 hours while her brother Tom takes 8 hours. How long would it take for Bridget and Tom to clean 2 houses together?

   Start by figuring out how much of a house each sibling can clean on his or her own. Bridget can clean the house in 12 hours, so she can clean $\frac{1}{12}$ of the house in an hour. Using the same logic, Tom can clean $\frac{1}{8}$ of a house in an hour.

   By adding these values together, you get the fraction of the house they can clean together in an hour:

   $\frac{1}{12} + \frac{1}{8} = \frac{5}{24}$

   They can do $\frac{5}{24}$ of the job per hour.

   Now set up variables and an equation to solve:

   t = time spent cleaning (in hours)

   h = number of houses cleaned = 2

   work = rate × time

   $h = \frac{5}{24} t \rightarrow$

   $2 = \frac{5}{24} t \rightarrow$

   $t = \frac{48}{5} = 9\frac{3}{5}$ **hours**

2. Farmer Dan needs to water his cornfield. One hose can water a field 1.25 times faster than a second hose. When both hoses are opened, they water the field in 5 hours. How long would it take to water the field if only the second hose is used?

   In this problem you don't know the exact time, but you can still find the hourly rate as a variable:

   The first hose completes the job in f hours, so it waters $\frac{1}{f}$ field per hour. The slower hose waters the field in 1.25f, so it waters the field in $\frac{1}{1.25f}$ hours. Together, they take 5 hours to water the field, so they water $\frac{1}{5}$ of the field per hour.

   Now you can set up the equations and solve:

$$\frac{1}{f} + \frac{1}{1.25f} = \frac{1}{5} \rightarrow$$

$$1.25f\left(\frac{1}{f} + \frac{1}{1.25f}\right) = 1.25f\left(\frac{1}{5}\right) \rightarrow$$

$$1.25 + 1 = 0.25f$$

$$2.25 = 0.25f$$

$$f = 9$$

The fast hose takes 9 hours to water the cornfield. The slower hose takes 1.25(9) = **11.25 hours**.

3. Alex takes 2 hours to shine 500 silver spoons, and Julian takes 3 hours to shine 450 silver spoons. How long will they take, working together, to shine 1000 silver spoons?

Calculate how many spoons each man can shine per hour:

Alex: $\dfrac{500 \text{ spoons}}{2 \text{ hours}} = \dfrac{250 \text{ spoons}}{1 \text{ hour}}$

Julian: $\dfrac{450 \text{ spoons}}{3 \text{ hours}} = \dfrac{150 \text{ spoons}}{1 \text{ hour}}$

Together: $\dfrac{250 + 150}{1 \text{ hour}} = \dfrac{400 \text{ spoons}}{1 \text{ hour}}$

Now set up an equation to find the time it takes to shine 1000 spoons:

total time $= \dfrac{1 \text{ hour}}{400 \text{ spoons}} \times 1000 \text{ spoons} = \dfrac{1000}{40} \text{ hours} = \textbf{2.5 hours}$

GRAPHS AND CHARTS

These questions require you to interpret information from graphs and charts; they will be pretty straightforward as long as you pay careful attention to detail. There are several different graph and chart types that may appear on the TABE.

Bar Graphs and Histograms

BAR GRAPHS present the numbers of an item that exist in different categories. The categories are shown on one axis, and the number of items is shown on the other axis. Bar graphs are usually used to easily compare amounts.

On the test you'll need to both read graphs and determine what kinds of graphs are appropriate for different situations.

Histograms similarly use bars to compare data, but the independent variable is a continuous variable that has been "binned" or divided into categories. For example, the time of day can be broken down into 8:00 a.m. to 12:00 p.m., 12:00 p.m. to 4:00 p.m., and so on. Usually (but not always), a gap is included between the bars of a bar graph but not a histogram.

Histograms can be symmetrical, skewed left or right, or multimodal (data spread around). Note that **SKEWED LEFT** means the peak of the data is on the *right*, with a tail to the left, while **SKEWED RIGHT** means the peak is on the *left*, with a tail to the right. This seems counterintuitive to many; the "left" or "right" always refers to the tail of the data. This is because a long tail to the right, for example, means there are high outlier values that are skewing the data to the right.

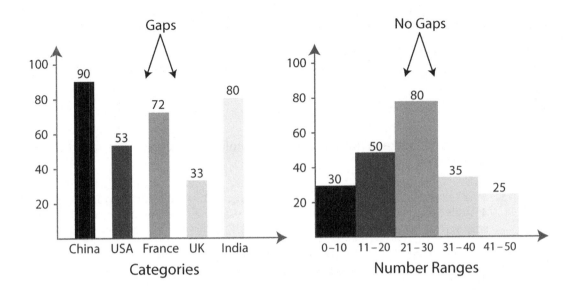

Bar Graph

Histogram

Figure 3.4. Bar Graph versus Histogram

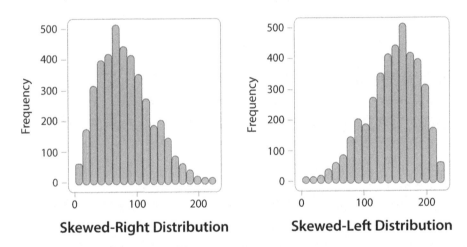

Skewed-Right Distribution

Skewed-Left Distribution

Figure 3.5. Histogram Skew

Examples

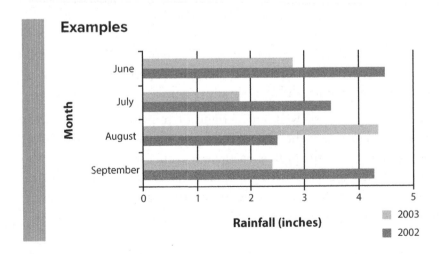

1. The graph above shows rainfall in inches per month. Which month had the least amount of rainfall? Which had the most?

The shortest bar represents the month with the least rain, and the longest bar represents the month with the most rain: **July 2003 had the least**, and **June 2002 had the most**.

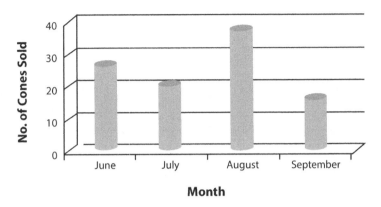

2. According to the graph above, how many more ice cream cones were sold in July than in September?

Tracing from the top of each bar to the scale on the left shows that sales in July were 20 and September sales were 15. So, **5 more cones were sold in July**.

Pie Charts

PIE CHARTS present parts of a whole and are often used with percentages. Together, all the slices of the pie add up to the total number of items, or 100%.

Examples

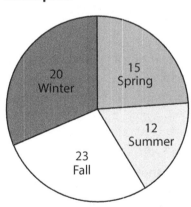

1. The pie chart above shows the distribution of birthdays in a class of students. How many students have birthdays in the spring or summer?

Fifteen students have birthdays in spring and 12 in summer, so there are **27 students** with birthdays in spring or summer.

2. Using the same Birthday Pie Chart in the example before, what percentage of students have birthdays in winter? Round to the nearest tenth of a percent.

Use the equation for percent:

$$percent = \frac{part}{whole} = \frac{winter\ birthdays}{total\ birthdays} =$$

$$\frac{20}{20 + 15 + 23 + 12} = \frac{20}{70} = \frac{2}{7} = .286\ or\ \mathbf{28.6\%}$$

Line Graphs

LINE GRAPHS show trends over time. The number of each item represented by the graph will be on the *y*-axis, and time will be on the *x*-axis.

Examples

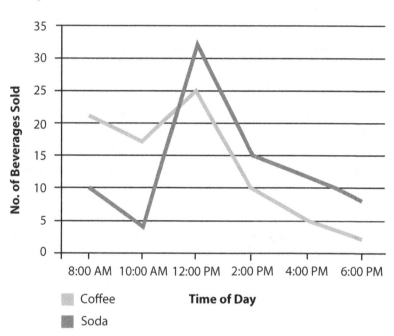

1. The line graph above shows beverage sales at an airport snack shop throughout the day. Which beverage sold more at 4:00 p.m.?

   At 4:00 p.m., approximately 12 sodas and 5 coffees were sold, so more **soda** was sold.

2. At what time of day were the most beverages sold?

   This question is asking for the time of day with the most sales of coffee and soda combined. It is not necessary to add up sales at each time of day to find the answer. Just from looking at the graph, you can see that sales for both beverages were highest at noon, so the answer must be **12:00 p.m**.

MEAN, MEDIAN, AND MODE

MEAN is a math term for average. To find the mean, total all the terms and divide by the number of terms. The **MEDIAN** is the middle number of a given set. To find the median, put the terms in numerical order; the middle number will be the median. In the case of a set of even numbers, the middle two numbers are averaged. **MODE** is the number which occurs most frequently within a given set.

Examples

1. Find the mean of 24, 27, and 18.

   Add the terms, then divide by the number of terms:

   $\text{mean} = \frac{24 + 27 + 18}{3} = \mathbf{23}$

2. The mean of three numbers is 45. If two of the numbers are 38 and 43, what is the third number?

   Set up the equation for mean with x representing the third number, then solve:

   $\text{mean} = \frac{38 + 43 + x}{3} = 45$

   $38 + 43 + x = 135$

   $\mathbf{x = 54}$

3. What is the median of 24, 27, and 18?

   Place the terms in order, then pick the middle term:

   18, 24, 27

   The median is 24.

4. What is the median of 24, 27, 18, and 19?

   Place the terms in order. Because there are an even number of terms, the median will be the average of the middle 2 terms:

   18, 19, 24, 27

   $\text{median} = \frac{19 + 24}{2} = \mathbf{21.5}$

5. What is the mode of 2, 5, 4, 4, 3, 2, 8, 9, 2, 7, 2, and 2?

   The mode is 2 because it appears the most within the set.

AREA AND PERIMETER

Most of the geometry problems on the TABE will require you to find either the area inside a shape or its perimeter (the distance around it). The perimeter is found by simply adding the lengths of all the sides. (Perimeter uses units for *length*, such as feet, inches, or meters. Because area is found by multiplying two lengths, it has units of *length squared*, such as square feet, ft², or square meters, m².) You will need to memorize the formula for the area of basic shapes, including triangles, rectangles, and circles.

Table 3.3. Area and Perimeter of Basic Shapes

SHAPE	EXAMPLE	AREA	PERIMETER
Triangle		$A = \frac{1}{2}bh$	$P = s_1 + s_2 + s_3$
Square		$A = s^2$	$P = 4s$

Table 3.3. Area and Perimeter of Basic Shapes (continued)

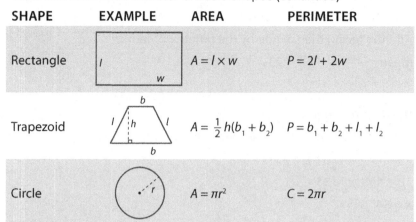

SHAPE	EXAMPLE	AREA	PERIMETER
Rectangle		$A = l \times w$	$P = 2l + 2w$
Trapezoid		$A = \frac{1}{2}h(b_1 + b_2)$	$P = b_1 + b_2 + l_1 + l_2$
Circle		$A = \pi r^2$	$C = 2\pi r$

The TABE will include area and perimeter problems with compound shapes. These are complex shapes made by combining more basic shapes. While they might look complicated, they can be solved by simply breaking the compound shape apart and using the formulas given above.

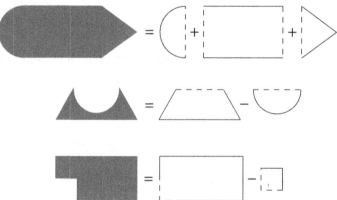

Figure 3.6. Compound Shapes

Examples

1. What is the area of the shaded region?

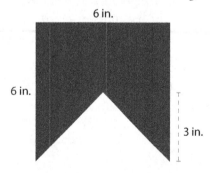

The figure is a square with a triangle cut out. First, find the area of the square:

$A = s^2 = 6^2 = 36$ in²

Now find the area of the triangle:

$A = \frac{1}{2}bh = \frac{1}{2}(6)(3) = 9$ in²

Subtract the area of the triangle from the area of the square:

36 – 9 = 27 in²

2. A farmer has purchased 100 m of fencing to put around his rectangular garden. If one side of the garden is 20 m long and the other is 28 m, how much fencing will the farmer have left over?

The perimeter of a rectangle is equal to twice its length plus twice its width:

$P = 2(20) + 2(28) = 96$ m

The farmer has 100 m of fencing, so subtract to find the amount of fence left:

100 – 96 = **4** m

PYTHAGOREAN THEOREM

Shapes with 3 sides are known as **TRIANGLES**. In addition to knowing the formulas for their area and perimeter, you should also know the Pythagorean theorem, which describes the relationship between the three sides (*a*, *b*, and *c*) of a right triangle:

$$a^2 + b^2 = c^2$$

Example

Erica is going to run a race in which she'll run 3 miles due north and 4 miles due east. She'll then run back to the starting line. How far will she run during this race?

One leg of her route (the triangle) is missing, but you can find its length using the Pythagorean theorem:

$a^2 + b^2 = c^2$

$3^2 + 4^2 = c^2$

$25 = c^2$

$c = 5$

Adding all 3 sides gives the length of the whole race:

3 + 4 + 5 = **12 miles**

TEST YOUR KNOWLEDGE

Work the problem, and then choose the most correct answer.

1. Melissa has been thinking about buying a car. She estimates that she would spend $200 per month on car payments, $25 per week on gas, and $600 per year on insurance. About how much would she spend per month? (Note: a month contains four weeks.)

    A) $125

    B) $275

    C) $350

    D) $825

2. Mary works from 5:00 p.m. to 8:30 p.m. on Wednesdays and Thursdays, and from 9:00 a.m. to 3:30 p.m. on Saturdays and Sundays. How many hours does Mary work per week?

    A) 10

    B) 14.5

    C) 18

    D) 20

3. A car rental company charges a daily fee of $48 plus 25% of the daily fee for every hour the car is late. If you rent a car for 2 days and bring it back 2 hours late, what will be the total charge?

    A) $72

    B) $108

    C) $120

    D) $144

4. Rebecca, Emily, and Kate all live on the same straight road. Rebecca lives 1.4 miles from Kate and 0.8 miles from Emily. What is the minimum distance Emily could live from Kate?

    A) 0.6 miles

    B) 0.8 miles

    C) 1.1 miles

    D) 2.2 miles

5. Alex, David, and Rachel go out to dinner. Alex and David decide to split an appetizer that costs $8.50, and Rachel gets her own appetizer that costs $6.50. Rachel also orders lemonade that costs $3. They all order entrées that cost the same price. They split up the bill according to what each person ordered; how much less (before tax and tip) will Alex and David each pay compared to Rachel?

    A) $1.00

    B) $5.00

    C) $5.25

    D) $7.25

6. During a recent storm, it snowed at a rate of 2 centimeters per hour for 190 minutes, 4 centimeters per hour for 40 minutes, 1 centimeter per hour for 280 minutes, and 3 millimeters per hour for 50 minutes. What was the total snowfall to the nearest centimeter?

    A) 10

    B) 13

    C) 14

    D) 16

7. A car dealership is offering a special deal: this year's models are 20% off the list price, and the dealership will pay the first 3 monthly payments. If a car is listed for $26,580, and the monthly payments are $250, how much would a customer save with this deal?

    A) $1,282

    B) $5,566

    C) $6,066

    D) $20,514

8. To get to work, Matt walks 0.75 miles from his house to the bus stop and rides the bus 3.8 miles to his office. If he walks at a pace of 3.6 miles per hour and the bus drives at an average speed of 15 miles per hour, how long is his commute?

   A) 27 minutes, 7 seconds

   B) 27 minutes, 42 seconds

   C) 46 minutes, 16 seconds

   D) 1 hour, 6 minutes, 20 seconds

9. There are 450 students in the 10th grade; of these, 46% are boys. If 21% of the girls have already turned 16, how many girls in the 10th grade are 16?

   A) 10

   B) 47

   C) 51

   D) 94

10. Joe baked brownies in a 9 inch by 11 inch by 2 inch pan. He then cut the brownies into 12 large pieces. Joe ate 2 pieces, his roommate ate 3 pieces, and the dog unfortunately ate half of what was remaining. How many cubic inches of brownies did the dog eat?

    A) 57.75

    B) 82.5

    C) 99

    D) 115.5

11. Which of the following numbers are integers?

I.	-7
II.	14.5
III.	$\sqrt{64}$

    A) I only

    B) II only

    C) I and III

    D) II and III

12. Which of the following is an irrational number?

    A) 1.085

    B) $\frac{\pi}{2}$

    C) $\frac{9}{5}$

    D) 16

13. What kind of number is $-\frac{\sqrt{4}}{17}$?

    A) whole number

    B) integer

    C) rational number

    D) irrational number

14. Simplify the following expression:
    $$\frac{-24(2)^{-1}}{-3}$$

    A) -16

    B) -4

    C) $\frac{1}{144}$

    D) 4

15. Simplify the following inequality:
    $30 - 9x > -6y$

    A) $y < -5 - \frac{2}{3}x$

    B) $y < -5 + \frac{2}{3}x$

    C) $y > -5 + \frac{2}{3}x$

    D) $y > 5 - \frac{2}{3}x$

16. Which of the following is true about negative numbers?

    A) A negative number raised to a negative number is a positive number.

    B) A negative number divided by the product of a negative number and a positive number is a positive number.

    C) The product of a negative number and a positive number, raised to a negative number, is a negative number.

    D) Both B and C

17. Solve $\dfrac{\left(\frac{35}{7}\right)^2 - 3^2}{7 + 1}$

A) 2

B) 20.7

C) 60.5

D) 54,227

18. Solve $(3 + 5)^2 + 24 ÷ 16 - 5 ÷ 2$

A) 0.25

B) 30.25

C) 33

D) 63

19. Which of the following expressions can be simplified to $8x$?

A) $10 - 2\left(\dfrac{x^2 - x}{x}\right) + 1$

B) $\left(\dfrac{6 + 9}{7 - 4}\right)x + 9 - 6x$

C) $\dfrac{48}{6 \times 4} + 2^3x - \dfrac{4^{(9-6)}}{32}$

D) $16\left(\dfrac{x^2}{2^{-1}}\right)$

20. Simplify the following expression:
$4 - \dfrac{1}{2^2} + 24 ÷ (8 + 12)$

A) 1.39

B) 2.74

C) 4.95

D) 15.28

21. Which of the following statements about order of operations is false?

A) Operations inside parentheses are simplified before operations outside parentheses.

B) Multiplication is completed before division.

C) Exponents are simplified before addition is completed.

D) Addition and subtraction are completed left to right.

22. Simplify: $\sqrt{(375 + 5^3) - (36 + 64)} - 8$

A) 4.36

B) 12

C) 14.98

D) 28

23. Which of the following expressions is equivalent to the expression $(2 \times x^2) - (y ÷ 3)^4 + 5 ÷ 8^2$?

A) $2(x^2 - y) ÷ 3^4 + \left(\dfrac{5}{8}\right)^2$

B) $(2x)^2 - \dfrac{y^4 + 5}{3 + 8^2}$

C) $2x^2 - \left(\dfrac{y}{3}\right)^4 + \left(\dfrac{5}{64}\right)$

D) $\dfrac{2x^2 - y}{3^4} + \dfrac{5}{64}$

24. Simplify: $[56 ÷ (2 \times 2^2)] - 9 ÷ 3$

A) -0.667

B) 4

C) 34.33

D) 109

25. Simplify: $3.819 + 14.68 + 0.0006$

A) 5.2846

B) 18.4996

C) 18.505

D) 52.96

26. Simplify: $59.09 - 5.007 - 6.21$

A) 47.792

B) 47.81

C) 47.873

D) 47.882

27. How many digits are in the sum $951.4 + 98.908 + 1.053$?

A) 4

B) 5

C) 6

D) 7

28. Simplify: $105.71 ÷ 31$

A) 0.341

B) 3.41

C) 34.1

D) 341

29. Simplify: $54.48 \div 0.6$
   A) 0.908
   B) 9.08
   C) 90.8
   D) 908

30. Simplify: 0.08×0.12
   A) 0.0096
   B) 0.096
   C) 0.96
   D) 9.6

31. $\frac{4}{9} \times \frac{1}{2} \times \frac{6}{4} =$
   A) $\frac{2}{9}$
   B) $\frac{1}{3}$
   C) $\frac{2}{3}$
   D) $\frac{64}{3}$

32. $\frac{8}{15}$ is $\frac{1}{6}$ of what number?
   A) $\frac{4}{45}$
   B) $\frac{15}{48}$
   C) $\frac{46}{15}$
   D) $\frac{16}{5}$

33. Simplify the expression: $5\frac{2}{3} \times 1\frac{7}{8} \div \frac{1}{3}$
   A) $3\frac{13}{24}$
   B) $6\frac{3}{4}$
   C) $15\frac{3}{4}$
   D) $31\frac{7}{8}$

34. Ali, Charlotte, and Katie are selling boxes of candy. The shipment of candy arrives at Ali's house; Ali gives $\frac{4}{15}$ of the boxes to Charlotte and $\frac{3}{10}$ of the boxes to Katie. What fraction of the original shipment is left for Ali?
   A) $\frac{3}{10}$
   B) $\frac{8}{15}$
   C) $\frac{13}{30}$
   D) $\frac{17}{30}$

35. Adam is shopping the clearance section at his favorite department store. He finds a jacket that is marked $\frac{1}{3}$ off. His student discount gives him an additional $\frac{1}{5}$ off the original price. By what fraction is the jacket discounted in total?
   A) $\frac{1}{15}$
   B) $\frac{6}{15}$
   C) $\frac{7}{15}$
   D) $\frac{8}{15}$

36. On Monday, Grace fills the gas tank of her car up to $\frac{3}{4}$ full. On Tuesday, she uses $\frac{1}{8}$ of a tank, on Wednesday she uses $\frac{3}{16}$ of a tank, and on Thursday she uses another $\frac{1}{4}$ of a tank. What fraction of the gas tank is full after Thursday?
   A) $\frac{3}{16}$
   B) $\frac{1}{4}$
   C) $\frac{7}{16}$
   D) $\frac{13}{16}$

37. Based on a favorable performance review at work, Matt receives a $\frac{3}{20}$ increase in his hourly wage. If his original hourly wage is represented by w, express his new wage in decimal form.

A) 0.15w

B) 0.85w

C) 1.12w

D) 1.15w

38. Express $\frac{15}{25}$ as a decimal.

A) 0.06

B) 0.15

C) 0.375

D) 0.6

39. How many cents is $\frac{8}{11}$ of a dollar?

A) 0.72

B) 0.73

C) 0.79

D) 0.81

40. Stephanie eats 0.625 of her pizza. If her pizza was cut into 8 slices, how many slices has she eaten?

A) 3

B) 4

C) 5

D) 6

41. A carnival game involves picking rubber ducks with numbers written on the bottom. There is a 0.05 probability of picking a rubber duck with the number 3. What fraction of the rubber ducks are numbered 3?

A) $\frac{1}{20}$

B) $\frac{3}{20}$

C) $\frac{1}{5}$

D) $\frac{1}{15}$

42. A chocolate chip cookie recipe calls for 2.375 cups of flour. Express this quantity as a fraction.

A) $2\frac{3}{5}$ cups

B) $2\frac{3}{8}$ cups

C) $2\frac{2}{8}$ cups

D) $2\frac{1}{3}$ cups

43. A marinade recipe calls for 2 tablespoons of lemon juice for $\frac{1}{4}$ cup of olive oil. How much lemon juice should you use with $\frac{2}{3}$ cup olive oil?

A) $5\frac{1}{3}$ tablespoons

B) $\frac{3}{4}$ tablespoons

C) 4 tablespoons

D) $2\frac{1}{3}$ tablespoons

44. A material's specific heat capacity is the amount of energy needed to increase the temperature of 1 gram of that material by 1 degree Celsius. If the specific heat capacity of aluminum is $0.900 \frac{J}{g \cdot {}^\circ C}$, how many joules of energy does it take to increase the temperature of 2 grams of aluminum by 4 degrees Celsius?

A) 3.6 joules

B) 0.1 joules

C) 7.2 joules

D) 5.6 joules

45. The density of cork is approximately 0.24 grams per cubic centimeter. How much water would 100 grams of cork displace?

A) 3.67 cm³

B) 1.24 cm³

C) 24 cm³

D) 4.17 cm³

46. Stephanie's car uses an average of 29 miles per gallon. $\frac{1}{3}$ of her gas tank holds 3.5 gallons. How many miles can she drive on a full tank of gas?

   A) 33.8 miles

   B) 101.5 miles

   C) 367.5 miles

   D) 304.5 miles

47. Adam owns 4 times as many shirts as he has pairs of pants, and he has 5 pairs of pants for every 2 pairs of shoes. What is the ratio of Adam's shirts to Adam's shoes?

   A) 25 shirts : 1 pair shoes

   B) 10 shirts : 1 pair shoes

   C) 20 shirts : 1 pair shoes

   D) 15 shirts : 2 pairs shoes

48. A box of instant rice provides the following instructions: "For 4 servings, stir 2 cups of rice into 1.75 cups of boiling water." How many cups of water are needed for 6 servings of rice?

   A) 2.625 cups

   B) 13.7 cups

   C) 3 cups

   D) 1.167 cups

49. A restaurant employs servers, hosts, and managers in a ratio of 9:2:1. If there are 36 total employees, how many hosts are there?

   A) 4

   B) 3

   C) 6

   D) 8

50. 7 is what percent of 60?

   A) 11.67%

   B) 4.20%

   C) 8.57%

   D) 10.11%

51. What percent of 14 is 35?

   A) 4.9%

   B) 2.5%

   C) 40%

   D) 250%

52. 15 is 8 percent of what number?

   A) 1.2

   B) 53.3

   C) 187.5

   D) 120

53. On a given day at the local airport, 15 flights were delayed and 62 left on time. What percentage of the flights was delayed?

   A) 24.2%

   B) 19.5%

   C) 80.5%

   D) 22.4%

54. Gym A offers a monthly membership for 80% of the cost at Gym B; the cost at Gym B is 115% the cost at Gym C. What percentage of the cost at Gym C does Gym A charge?

   A) 35%

   B) 97%

   C) 70%

   D) 92%

55. If there are 380 female students in a graduating class, and male students represent 60% of the graduating class, how many total students are there in the class?

   A) 633

   B) 950

   C) 570

   D) 720

56. What is 18% of 76% of 15,000?

   A) 3,553

   B) 2,052

   C) 633

   D) 8,700

57. A manufacturer sells a product to a retailer for 350% of the production cost. The retailer sells the product to consumers for 600% of the production cost. What percentage of her purchase cost is the retailer's profit when she sells to consumers?

A) 250%

B) 41.7%

C) 58.3%

D) 71.4%

58. Evaluate the expression $\frac{4x}{x-1}$ when $x = 5$.

A) 3

B) 4

C) 5

D) 6

59. Evaluate the expression $\frac{x^2 - 2y}{y}$ when $x = 20$ and $y = \frac{x}{2}$.

A) 0

B) 38

C) 36

D) 19

60. Evaluate the expression $\sqrt{(x^{-1})4x}$ when $x = y + 3$ and $y = 14$.

A) 2

B) −2

C) 34

D) $\frac{1}{\sqrt{2}}$

61. Simplify: $3x^3 + 4x - (2x + 5y) + y$

A) $3x^3 + 2x + y$

B) $11x - 4y$

C) $3x^3 + 2x - 4y$

D) $29x - 4y$

62. Find the sum: $2\left(\frac{y}{x}\right) + \frac{1}{x}(3y)$

A) $\frac{y}{x}$

B) $\frac{5y}{x^2}$

C) $\frac{5y}{6x}$

D) $\frac{5y}{x}$

63. Simplify the expression:
$x^3 - 3x^2 + (2x)^3 - x$

A) $x^3 - 3x^2 + 7x$

B) $9x^3 - 3x^2 - x$

C) $20x$

D) $7x^3 - 3x^2 - x$

64. What is the range of the function $f(x) = x^2 + 2$?

A) all real numbers

B) all real numbers greater than 2

C) all real numbers greater than or equal to 2

D) all real numbers less than or equal to 2

65. Consider the function $f(x) = -2x - 5$ with the range {17, 15, 11, −5}. Define the domain.

A) domain = {−11, −10, −8, 0}

B) domain = {−39, −35, −27, 5}

C) domain = {−14, −11, −6, 0}

D) domain = {−6, −5, −3, 5}

66. Which of the following is always true of functions?

A) For each value in the range, there is only one value in the domain.

B) For each value in the domain, there is only one value in the range.

C) The range of a function includes all real numbers.

D) The domain of a function includes all real numbers.

67. If $f(x) = 3^x - 2$, evaluate $f(5)$.

A) 27

B) 243

C) 241

D) 13

68. Which of the following is true of the function $(x) = 8^x$?

A) The graph of the function has a horizontal asymptote along the negative *x*-axis.

B) The graph of the function has a horizontal asymptote along the positive *x*-axis.

C) The graph of the function has a vertical asymptote along the negative *y*-axis.

D) The graph of the function has a vertical asymptote along the positive *y*-axis.

69. If $f(x) = 0.5^x + 1$, evaluate $f(-2)$.

A) 0.75

B) 2

C) 4

D) 5

70. If $f(x) = e^{2x}$, evaluate $\ln[f(3)]$.

A) 3

B) 5

C) 6

D) $\frac{1}{e^6}$

71. Which of the following is true of the function $f(x) = 1^x - 3$?

A) The graph of the function is a horizontal line at $y = -2$.

B) The graph of the function is a vertical line at $x = -2$.

C) The graph of the function has a horizontal asymptote at $y = -3$.

D) The graph of the function has a vertical asymptote at $x = -3$.

72. A 650 square foot apartment in Boston costs $1800 per month to rent. What is the monthly rent per square foot?

A) $13

B) $0.36

C) $2.77

D) $3.66

73. A radio station plays songs that last an average of 3.5 minutes and has commercial breaks that last 2 minutes. If the station is required to play 1 commercial break for every 4 songs, how many songs can the station play in an hour?

A) 15

B) 11

C) 16

D) 17

74. Students in a particular math class received an average score of 84% on a recent test. If there are 20 boys and 30 girls in the class, and the boys' average score was 82%, what was the girls' average score?

A) 83%

B) 88%

C) 85%

D) 86%

75. $\frac{1}{10}$ of a company's employees are in their 20s, $\frac{2}{5}$ are in their 30s, $\frac{1}{3}$ are in their 40s and the remaining 5 employees are 50 or older. How many employees work at the company?

A) 5

B) 30

C) 60

D) 24

76. A chemical experiment requires that a solute be diluted with 4 parts (by mass) water for every 1 part (by mass) solute. If the desired mass for the solution is 90 grams, how much solute should be used?

A) 15 grams

B) 72 grams

C) 22.5 grams

D) 18 grams

77. Lisa rides her bike at 10 miles per hour for 28 minutes, 15 miles per hour for 49 minutes, and 12 miles per hour for 15 minutes. How far did she travel in total?

A) 11.95 miles

B) 18.91 miles

C) 19.92 miles

D) 20.21 miles

78. A plane makes a trip of 246 miles. For some amount of time, the plane's speed is 115 miles per hour. For the remainder of the trip, the plane's speed is 250 miles per hour. If the total trip time is 72 minutes, how long did the plane fly at 115 miles per hour?

A) 18 minutes

B) 23 minutes

C) 24 minutes

D) 34 minutes

79. A runner completes a 12 mile race in 1 hour and 30 minutes. If her pace for the first part of the race was 7 minutes per mile, and her pace for the second part of the race was 8 minutes per mile, for how many miles did she sustain her pace of 7 minutes per mile?

A) 4 miles

B) 5.5 miles

C) 6 miles

D) 7 miles

80. A swimmer is swimming 25 meter sprints. If he swims 4 sprints in 3 minutes, 6 more sprints in 5 minutes, and then 4 final sprints in 2 minutes, what was his average speed during his sprints?

A) 35 meters per minute

B) 1.4 meters per minute

C) 350 meters per minute

D) 17.9 meters per minute

81. A cheetah in the wild can accelerate from 0 miles per hour to 60 miles per hour in 2.8 seconds. Then, it can sustain a speed of 60 miles per hour for up to 60 seconds before it has to rest. How much total distance can the cheetah travel from when it starts to accelerate to the moment it has to stop?

A) 3,684 miles

B) 2.4 miles

C) 1.046 miles

D) 1.023 miles

82. 2 warehouse workers can pack 5 boxes in 6 minutes. If 1 worker can pack 6 boxes by himself in 15 minutes, how many boxes can the other worker pack by himself in the same amount of time?

A) 6.5 boxes

B) 6 boxes

C) 12.5 boxes

D) 7.5 boxes

83. John and Jake are working at a car wash. It takes John 1 hour to wash 3 cars; Jake can wash 3 cars in 45 minutes. If they work together, how many cars can they wash in 1 hour?

A) 6 cars

B) 7 cars

C) 9 cars

D) 12 cars

84. Ed is going to fill his swimming pool with a garden hose. His neighbor, a volunteer firefighter, wants to use a fire hose attached to the hydrant in the front yard to make the job go faster. The fire hose sprays 13.5 times as much water per minute as the garden hose. If the garden hose and the fire hose together can fill the pool in 107 minutes, how long would it have taken to fill the pool with the garden hose alone?

A) 7 hours, 37.9 min

B) 7 hours, 55.6 min

C) 1 day, 4.5 min

D) 1 day, 1 hour, 51.5 min

85. Suppose Mark can mow the entire lawn in 47 minutes, and Mark's dad can mow the entire lawn in 53 minutes. If Mark and his dad work together (each with their own lawnmowers), how long will it take them to mow the entire lawn?

A) 15.6 minutes

B) 24.9 minutes

C) 26.5 minutes

D) 50 minutes

86. Rafael and Marco are repainting their garage. If Rafael can paint $\frac{1}{6}$ of the garage in 20 minutes, and Marco can paint $\frac{1}{5}$ of the garage in 30 minutes, how long will it take them to paint the entire garage if they work together?

A) 1 hr, 6.7 min

B) 2 hr, 43.6 min

C) 0 hr, 54 min

D) 6 hr, 12 min

87. Find the area of a rectangular athletic field that is 100 meters long and 45 meters wide.

A) 290 meters

B) 4,500 m²

C) 145 m²

D) 4.5 km²

88. Melissa is ordering fencing to enclose a square area of 5625 square feet. How many feet of fencing does she need?

A) 75 feet

B) 150 feet

C) 300 feet

D) 5,625 feet

89. Adam is painting a 4-walled shed. The shed is 5 feet wide, 4 feet deep, and 7 feet high. How much paint will Adam need?

A) 126 ft²

B) 140 ft³

C) 63 ft²

D) 46 feet

90. James is building an octagonal gazebo with equal sides in his backyard. If one side is 5.5 feet wide, what is the perimeter of the entire gazebo?

A) 22 feet

B) 30.25 feet

C) 44 feet

D) 242 feet

91. A courtyard garden has flower beds in the shape of 4 equilateral triangles arranged so that their bases enclose a square space in the middle for a fountain. If the space for the fountain has an area of 1 square meter, find the total area of the flower beds and fountain space.

A) 1.73 m²

B) 2.73 m²

C) 1.43 m²

D) 3 m²

92. 2 identical circles are drawn next to each other with their sides just touching; both circles are enclosed in a rectangle whose sides are tangent to the circles. If each circle's radius is 2 inches, find the area of the rectangle.

A) 24 cm²

B) 8 cm²

C) 32 cm²

D) 16 cm²

93. A grain silo is cylinder-shaped with a height of 10 meters and a diameter of 3.2 meters. What is the surface area of the silo, including the top but not the base?

A) 233.23 m²

B) 265.40 m²

C) 116.61 m²

D) 108.57 m²

94. Find the total surface area of a box that is 12 inches long, 18 inches wide, and 6 inches high.

A) 144 in²

B) 1,296 in³

C) 792 in²

D) 396 in²

95. A developer is designing a rectangular parking lot for a new shopping center. A 20-foot-wide driving lane circles the interior, which has 6 rows of parking spaces divided by 5 driving lanes. Each row of parking spaces is 36 feet wide and 90 feet long. The driving lanes are 20 feet wide and 90 feet long. What is the perimeter of the entire parking lot?

A) 972 feet

B) 486 feet

C) 812 feet

D) 852 feet

96. A cylindrical canister is 9 inches high and has a diameter of 5 inches. What is the maximum volume this canister can hold?

A) 176.7 in²

B) 45 in²

C) 141.4 in²

D) 706.9 in²

97. If a spherical water balloon is filled with 113 milliliters of water, what is the approximate radius of the balloon?

A) 4.0 centimeters

B) 3.0 centimeters

C) 3.6 centimeters

D) 3.3 centimeters

98. A circular swimming pool has a circumference of 49 feet. What is the diameter of the pool?

A) 15.6 feet

B) 12.3 feet

C) 7.8 feet

D) 17.8 feet

99. A pizza has a diameter of 10 inches. If you cut a slice with a central angle of 40 degrees, how many inches of crust does that slice include?

A) 31.4 inches

B) 7.0 inches

C) 3.5 inches

D) 3.3 inches

100. A pizza has a diameter of 10 inches. If you cut a slice with a central angle of 40 degrees, what will be the surface area of the pizza slice?

A) 9.2 in²

B) 8.7 in²

C) 3.5 in²

D) 17.4 in²

101. Liz is installing a tile backsplash. If each tile is an equilateral triangle with sides that measure 6 centimeters in length, how many tiles does she need to cover an area of 1800 square centimeters?

A) 36 tiles

B) 100 tiles

C) 50 tiles

D) 300 tiles

102. The perimeter of an isosceles triangle is 25 centimeters. If the legs are twice as long as the base, what is the length of the base?

A) 5 centimeters

B) 10 centimeters

C) 15 centimeters

D) 8.3 centimeters

103. Meg rolled a 6-sided die 4 times, and her first 3 rolls were 1, 3, and 5. If the average of the 4 rolls is 2.5, what was the result of her fourth roll?

A) 1

B) 2

C) 3

D) 5

Use the table below to answer questions 104 and 105.

EMPLOYEE	HOURS WORKED
Olivia	42
Ben	38
Shawn	25
Ellen	50
Sophia	45
Ethan	46
Lilly	17
Noah	41

104. The table shows the number of hours worked by employees during the week. What is the median number of hours worked per week by the employees?

A) 38

B) 41

C) 42

D) 41.5

105. The table shows the number of hours worked by employees during the week. What is the difference between the median and mean number of hours worked per week?

A) 38

B) 3.5

C) 1.5

D) 41.5

106. A data set contains n points with a mean of μ. If a new data point with the value x is included in the data set, which of the following expressions is equal to the new mean?

A) $\dfrac{\mu + x}{n}$

B) $\dfrac{\mu n + x}{n + 1}$

C) $\dfrac{\mu n + x}{n}$

D) $\dfrac{(\mu + x)n}{n + 1}$

107. The average height of female students in a class is 64.5 inches, and the average height of male students in the class is 69 inches. If there are 1.5 times as many female students as male students, what is the average height for the entire class?

A) 67.2 inches

B) 66.75 inches

C) 67.5 inches

D) 66.3 inches

108. What is the probability of selecting a queen of hearts or a queen of diamonds from a normal deck of 52 playing cards?

A) $\dfrac{1}{2704}$

B) $\dfrac{1}{104}$

C) $\dfrac{1}{26}$

D) $\dfrac{1}{52}$

109. There are 3 red, 4 blue, and 6 black marbles in a bag. When Carlos reaches into the bag and selects a marble without looking, what are the chances that he will select a black marble?

A) 0.46

B) 0.86

C) 0.31

D) 0.23

Use the table below to answer question 110.

STUDENT	GRADE	NUMBER OF INSTRUMENTS
Alison	7	2
Dana	10	0
Clark	7	1
Sam	7	1
Luke	10	1
Philip	7	2
Briana	10	1
Laura	10	0
Angie	7	2

110. The data set shows number of instruments played by students in the 7th and 10th grades. What is the difference in the average number of instruments played by 7th- and 10th-graders?

A) 2.1

B) 1

C) 0.9

D) 0.5

111. Which of the following is a measure of central tendency that is most affected by an outlier in the data set?

A) mean

B) median

C) mode

D) range

112. Which of the following measures of central tendency changes when a constant is added to every data point in a data set?

A) mean

B) median

C) mode

D) all of the above

Answer Key

1.	C)	39.	B)	77.	C)
2.	D)	40.	C)	78.	C)
3.	C)	41.	A)	79.	C)
4.	A)	42.	B)	80.	A)
5.	C)	43.	A)	81.	D)
6.	C)	44.	C)	82.	A)
7.	C)	45.	D)	83.	B)
8.	B)	46.	D)	84.	D)
9.	C)	47.	B)	85.	B)
10.	A)	48.	A)	86.	A)
11.	D)	49.	C)	87.	B)
12.	B)	50.	A)	88.	C)
13.	D)	51.	D)	89.	A)
14.	D)	52.	C)	90.	C)
15.	C)	53.	B)	91.	B)
16.	D)	54.	D)	92.	C)
17.	A)	55.	B)	93.	D)
18.	D)	56.	B)	94.	C)
19.	C)	57.	D)	95.	A)
20.	C)	58.	C)	96.	A)
21.	B)	59.	B)	97.	B)
22.	B)	60.	A)	98.	A)
23.	C)	61.	C)	99.	C)
24.	B)	62.	D)	100.	B)
25.	B)	63.	B)	101.	B)
26.	C)	64.	C)	102.	A)
27.	D)	65.	A)	103.	A)
28.	B)	66.	B)	104.	D)
29.	C)	67.	C)	105.	B)
30.	A)	68.	A)	106.	B)
31.	B)	69.	D)	107.	D)
32.	D)	70.	C)	108.	C)
33.	D)	71.	A)	109.	A)
34.	C)	72.	C)	110.	C)
35.	D)	73.	A)	111.	A)
36.	A)	74.	C)	112.	D)
37.	D)	75.	B)		
38.	D)	76.	D)		

Made in the USA
Coppell, TX
11 April 2023

15488543R00057